TARNISHED DREAMS

Also by Jeanette Lukowski

Heart Scars

TARNISHED DREAMS

JEANETTE LUKOWSKI

Parents never stop
loving their children.
Jeanette

NORTH STAR PRESS OF ST. CLOUD, INC.
St. Cloud, Minnesota

My children helped me
figure out what
unconditional love is.
Thank you.

ISBN: 978-0-87839-723-5

First Edition: June 2014

Printed in the United States of America.

Published by
North Star Press of St. Cloud, Inc.
P.O. Box 451
St. Cloud, Minnesota 56302
northstarpress.com

Author's Note:

All of the events are true—but are re-told from my notes and memories.
Once again, I've made the decision to change the names of everyone else involved, to honor their right to privacy.

Table of Contents

PROLOGUE

IN APRIL 2009, my fifteen-year-old daughter, Allison, ran away from home. I knew I wasn't the first parent to experience the shock of discovering her child had run away—but I was the first in my family.

I was seventeen when my dad called me a slut; he caught me kissing my nineteen-year-old boyfriend good-bye on our back porch. I was hurt, but I didn't run away. A few weeks later, when my dad headed down the hall to get his hammer to break my bedroom door down (I was holding the door closed from the inside), I didn't run away. Instead, I escaped, staying at a friend's house until my mom moved my dad to a nursing home.

I understand pressures on a teenage girl, but I never ran away from home. Instead, I hid in a bottle of alcohol. I didn't need to run away from home; "home" had already abandoned me. My sister was away at college, and my mom was busy working three jobs. In addition, my mom made weekly visits to the nursing home—to exchange my dad's dirty laundry for clean clothes, to bring him a carton of cigarettes for the week, and to give him some cash for the vending machines. My role morphed into housewife—to an empty house. I washed my own laundry, kept the house clean, and prepared for dinner for two—which my mother would eat cold, perhaps, when she finally returned home.

THE FIRST DAYS after Allison returned home, I was grateful. As the days turned into weeks, I floated on happy thoughts, appreciative of every smile she granted me or giggle she let slip out. Spring became summer;

summer became fall; fall became winter. I couldn't stop thinking about the local police officer involved in the case. I couldn't stop thanking God for bringing my little girl back home. I even hugged Allison extra tight as we approached, and then passed, the one-year anniversary of that April weekend, the weekend that changed my life forever.

Somewhere after that first year, I began to relax. I stopped hearing every sound Allison made, I stopped worrying about her when she rounded a corner out of my sight, I stopped watching for miniscule changes in her behavior. I thought she had learned how dangerous life could be.

I WROTE *HEART SCARS* for myself. I needed to understand why Allison ran away from home.

Part of writing *Tarnished Dreams* was for you, my reader. Not because I want you to hate Allison, or applaud me for being such a terrific mother. (*I* don't, and I'm *not*.) I wrote it because two very interesting things happened during the first month of my book tour with *Heart Scars* the summer of 2013:

1) People constantly asked, "How is she now?"

2) I attended an event where a popular male writer of fiction spoke to a group of perhaps 100 people. I was sitting in the back row, interested in what he would say. Instead of speaking on his own agenda, he invited questions from the audience. I was unprepared for the answer to one of those questions.

"I was wondering if you have ever written about a difficult time in your life, and how you handled it."

The author began his answer, "We took in this fifteen-year-old girl one summer—she had run away from home. I think it's just a shame when parents decide they no longer want . . ."

I couldn't hear the rest of his answer, because the blood was rushing to my face. Sitting in the back row, I began quietly fuming about the man's overgeneralization.

Did I hear you correctly? Are you actually blaming the parents for this girl's behavior? Did you even know their *side?*

Earlier in the day, Tommy told me about Allison's latest post on her social networking site. "She says she's no longer couch-surfing," Tommy reported. "Instead, she says she's family-surfing."

"What do you mean? I don't understand what family-surfing means."

"She's staying with other people's families."

Just like the author in the front of the room was describing.

What *does* Allison tell the people who let her stay in their homes?

While I cannot say this is true for every fifteen-year-old (or eighteen-, or nineteen-, or twenty-year-old) who is homeless, I've come to the conclusion that *my* daughter does *exactly* what she *wants* to do.

I'VE ALSO WRITTEN this for me. The work of writing two memoirs helped me understand more about who *I* am—as I struggle with who I want to be in the future.

I've run through the first-date scenario in my head over the years, wanting to be ready if the occasion ever arose. The fantasy becomes a nightmare when he asks, "What do you like to do?"

I've never had an answer. I lost track of Jeanette.

Part One

Snapshots

One

The Envelope

IN FEBRUARY 2011, Allison was seventeen years old. Out of the blue, she asked to send her dad an email. Her request made me pause, since none of us had spoken to Frank since returning from Chicago in April 2009.

"I want to tell Dad what he has to do if he wants to have a relationship with me," Allison explained. "I'm willing to give him one more chance, but he's going to have to . . ."

The list was short, but direct. I admit I didn't pay too much attention to Allison's list of conditions, as I don't moderate the relationship with her father. I was impressed with her new display of assertiveness, though.

WHEN WE FIRST DIVORCED, I tried to honor the "rules" of divorce. Psychologists say it is important for children of divorce to have relationships with each parent, no matter how the parents feel about each other—so I set my resolve to letting the children spend time with their father whenever he was interested in having them.

The day he moved out, though, he invited me and the children over to his new apartment for dinner. It seemed too creepy for me, to head over to his new apartment for a dinner of take-out sub sandwiches hours after he left the house we had shared as a family, so I made up an excuse why we couldn't. I worried, too, about the children getting confused. Would the four-year-old think she was going to move into the apartment as well? Would the two-year-old make too much noise, running through long, perhaps empty apartment halls?

If he wanted to play family, why had Frank moved out?

I politely declined the invitation; Frank didn't talk to us for a week.

A month later, Frank asked to have the children for a day.

I invited Frank to spend Christmas Eve with us that year. It had been a month since he'd last seen the kids. My sister and I prepared an Italian dinner, and I set the dining room table like it was a restaurant table. It broke my heart when I realized Frank had snuck out to the garage to smoke a joint an hour after he walked into the house. He couldn't even spend time with his children sober.

Two weeks later, Frank came over to the house in a rage. He had been served the divorce papers—and tried to punch my face through the screen door's window. When that didn't work, he broke the picture frame we had given him as a Christmas gift—a collage frame with five different pictures of the children. Breaking the frame was one thing; shattering the frame's glass into their sandbox was another. But when he intentionally drove his car into the garage door before backing out of the driveway at full-speed, I got really scared. I called an organization that helps battered women, and borrowed a home-alarm security device. A single mother with two small children needed restful sleep in order to survive.

The next four months were unnerving. There were numerous nights Frank would call in a rage, and try to scare me enough to cancel the divorce proceedings. When he left one of those messages on the home's answering machine, I pulled the cassette tape out and moved it to the safe deposit box I had opened at the bank. I thought I might need it some day, if he ever pursued custody of our children—or my mother would need it, if I were murdered.

One night in March of 1998, Frank called to tell me he was sitting in the car, in the garage of his apartment building, with the engine running. He said he was going to kill himself. His threat of driving into a bridge abutment the week before hadn't resulted in my canceling the divorce, nor had his call while experiencing drug-induced hallucinations the week before, so I figured calling me from the car in the garage was just his latest attempt at manipulation.

Somehow, Frank ended up in a drug-rehab center after the car-in-garage incident. He called me from the center, wanting a ride back to his apartment. While I wanted to help him out—because I still loved the man who had been my husband—I feared the man he had become. What if he did something like Tom Cruise's character did in the movie *Vanilla Sky*? Frank could have easily grabbed the steering wheel of the car while I drove the two hours back to town; we would have died together, as a family, just like so many other violent husbands have done.

A month later, Frank moved back to Chicago. He called the morning of our appointment for divorce court, and asked for a ride to Minneapolis. A ninety-minute drive, so he could jump on a commercial bus.

Why couldn't he just tell me he loved me?

Why couldn't he just tell me he would change, and *mean* it this time?

Why couldn't he just stay in the area for the kids?

Frank called once a month for the first several months, but then even that stopped. Visits took place once every two or three years when I could afford to drive to Chicago; they were unsupervised until the kids shared snippets of their most recent visit a month later.

"I'm real good at taking care of Tommy, Mommy," eight-year-old Allison reported one day walking through the grocery store. "Daddy left us home alone while he ran out to get batteries. I was scared, but he was only gone like ten minutes."

"He left you alone, in his apartment?"

"It's okay," Allison continued. "We were watching movies."

"I got so scared after watching *Jurassic Park III*," six-year-old Tommy shared. "I tried to crawl into bed with Daddy, but he got angry because that meant his friend would have to move."

WHEN ALLISON RAN AWAY from home in 2009, she hadn't seen her dad for more than four years. The hour-long visit in the hospital in Chicago was meant to re-connect Frank and Allison, but Frank's weekly calls to Allison's cell phone drifted off again almost as soon as they began. By February 2011, we were approaching another two-year marker of not seeing him, and perhaps six months without a phone call.

AS THE CHILDREN got older, I tuned into the "How to be a Good Parent" pieces of advice, which included checking your children's email account. I struggled with the idea, recalling how I felt when my own parents found and read the notes I passed back and forth with a classmate in eighth grade choir class—and how their reading those notes began part of my downward spiral of: 1) not trusting my parents, and 2) not writing. Trust for my mother returned over the years, incrementally; feeling the freedom to write again took nearly four decades.

I also struggled with the idea because confronting Allison didn't change anything. Allison liked to intentionally create drama. During our day in court in 2010, I first heard about her story-telling reputation. Gregory's father had been questioned by the police after Allison ran away from home in April 2009; the defense attorney had a segment of the tape recording included in the trial, rather than putting Gregory's father on the stand. On the tape, Gregory's father was heard saying, "She's always telling stories. Everyone knows it! Greg knows it, Kale knows it—everyone knows it."

After Allison ran away in 2009, I found—and read—the few pages of journaling she had left behind in her room. In one journal, Allison wrote about letting a boy touch her breasts in the racquetball court of the Rec Center while I was watching her brother's basketball game in the gym. She was twelve; we lived in Wyoming at the time.

The idea disgusted me, but I couldn't imagine it being true. The Rec Center was too busy. The racquetball courts had glass walls into the corridor, so people could stand in the hall and watch.

A few pages later, I read about a "boy" she met online. According to Allison's journal, they had cyber sex together. There were no descriptions—just the phrase. She was thirteen at the time.

Another notebook, more information. At the age of fourteen, she met another "boy" online. She wanted to run away to live with him and his mom; they would be married when she turned sixteen. I think this boy was actually Jamie, the forty-year-old online predator who faked his own death while we were still in Wyoming.

I tried talking to Allison about topics in her journal from a therapist's approach, but never got her cooperation. "What do you think might happen to a young woman who . . ." the conversations began.

Sometimes, Allison would engage. "Yeah, like Rosie at school who . . ." or, "Kari told me about her cousin who . . ." Other times, Allison would blow me off. "Where did you get that dumb stuff from, Mom? One of those stupid talk shows? Like they have a clue."

It seemed like everything I tried always turned into a fight with Allison. Worse, nothing I did seemed to make Allison stop. Reading about them, though, made me ill. I never wanted to read her journals, or emailed conversations, unless I had to.

THE 2010-2011 ACADEMIC year was especially tough for me, as the country's economy took a dive. I was trying to hold everything together by working three part-time teaching jobs, and began working with a new school in January 2011. Mid-February, I was sitting in a shared office of the newest school, holding my required office hour after class, bored. No papers to grade, no colleagues to talk to, no book to read. Just me, a computer, and a chair.

I checked my email. No new messages.

I signed into my blog, but had no idea what to write about.

Forty-five more minutes to sit. I was so bored. Then I remembered Allison's comment about sending her father an email. I was bored, curious, and had a computer in front of me.

I was surprised to discover Allison hadn't changed the password to the account we had created together when she was younger. I was naïve to think she still only had the one Internet account.

Nothing new in her mailbox. Sadly, it didn't surprise me. Frank had always been solipsistic.

Or, did Allison really dig into him with claws this time? Waffling between not wanting to violate Allison's privacy by reading emails she exchanged with her father, but worrying about the lies she might be telling him, I opened the "Sent" box.

There it was, another Allison story. She told her father she was cutting, drinking, doing drugs. She, Tommy, and I were always fighting.

No wonder Frank hasn't replied. He's probably waiting to pounce on me.

Before signing out of her email account, I noticed a number of other email addresses in her "Sent" box. I also noticed the paperclip icon next to these addresses, which meant Allison sent attachments.

I opened the first one, and a picture box popped up. The picture box was approximately half an inch tall and half an inch wide, so it was very hard to see the image. I saw enough, though, to recognize Allison's face in the picture. Allison had sent this person a picture of herself.

Allison had sent *several* guys the same picture of herself.

I was angry, having worked so hard to keep my children's pictures off the Internet. I'd seen so many programs and public service announcements on TV over the years, warning viewers about online pedophiles, that I'd never even granted schools permission to use my children's pictures in online venues once schools began advertising that way. I was angry because Allison han't seemed to learn from her mistakes. (I would later discover Allison has *numerous* social networking sites.)

Hoping to get rid of these guys, I decided to forward the emails to my own email account. I sent emails warning the guys about the risks of contacting my underage daughter again from my own email account. But not all of the guys received only the profile picture; one guy received four pictures.

The thumbnails of the photographs were small and grainy. I couldn't quite see what Allison was wearing in two of the pictures.

I looked closer.

My stomach turned.

The bile rose up to my throat.

My hand shook so badly it took an extra second or two to get the email message to close.

I sat back; I tried to slow the racing of my heart through deep, steady breaths.

Was Allison topless in the one picture?

Why would my beautiful, quiet, little eleventh-grader send topless photos of herself to some guy?

The drive home was horrible. I couldn't figure out what to say to Allison when I picked her up from school—and I didn't want to have the conversation in front of Tommy.

I was sick to my stomach every time I thought about what Allison had done.

I NEVER FIGURED out how to talk to Allison about the emails before she announced her desire to get the mail from the mailbox at the end of our driveway. Daniel, her boyfriend of nine months, had apparently mailed her something special, and she wanted to check the mailbox at the end of our driveway every day until she got it. Rather than fight, I told Allison she could. What Allison *didn't* know was I screened the mail first. Every day, for a week, I swung by the house during the day, removed the mail from the mailbox, flipped through the pile to look at both the sender and recipient information, then put the pile back in the mailbox for Allison to take out later.

I forgot about the arrangement by the second week, though, and removed the entire stack from the mailbox on Monday.

Flipping through the stack of mail at a stoplight, I spotted an envelope that made my heart skip a beat. It was a plain white, four-by-nine-inch envelope, addressed to Allison—but I didn't recognize the name in the return address. It was coming from someplace in California. Was this from the guy she emailed the four pictures?

As I drove back to work, the wheels in my brain turned.

Allison was up to something again, and I was nervous. I couldn't help but imagine what the envelope contained, and it made me sick to my stomach.

I began thinking about possible courses of action, hoping to keep Allison safe:

#1) Text Allison and ask her what the hell she was doing. I didn't like to text her during school, though, and this would take too many rounds of question-and-answer texts to get anywhere. I also didn't want to upset her too much because she had a choir concert that night. Allison complained about migraines when she got too stressed; a migraine would make it difficult to sing in the choir concert; choir concerts were school-graded activities.

#2) Pull out my pen, write "Return to Sender" across the front of the envelope, drive it over to the post office, and deposit it in the outgoing mail slot. But if I did that, wouldn't the sender just call/text /email Allison and ask what happened? I wanted the contact with him to end, not just have her mad at me and potentially run away to meet him like she had when she was fifteen.

#3) Rip the envelope open and see what is inside. My gut told me I didn't want to see what was inside the envelope, though. And after all of the years spent watching police dramas on television, I was afraid to open it because that action might break whatever chain of forensic evidence the police would need if they investigated who sent Allison the envelope—and why.

When the ten-year-old girl in my neighborhood cut her forehead on the brick wall of another neighbor's house while several of us were playing a game with an empty cardboard refrigerator box, I calmly scooped the girl up in my arms, told another one of the kids to run ahead to notify her parents, and carried her down the block to her home.

When the store lights of the fabric store I worked for went out in 1984, I calmly walked to the back of the store, opened the stock room, saw it was on fire, and quietly told customers to leave the store.

When the tornado sirens went off in the summer of 1996, and I had to transport the children to the basement by myself—Frank was working—I calmly woke them up, got one in each arm, and carried them down the stairs. When the lights went out, and we listened to the trees falling all around us, I sang "Amazing Grace" as loud as I could.

But when I saw the envelope addressed to Allison, with a stranger's name in the return address corner, I realized I needed to talk with someone. I needed someone else to calmly tell me what to do.

I drove over to church, to talk with my pastor.

"What are you most scared of?" the pastor asked. "Are you scared for you? For Allison? But you really have to turn that envelope in."

I left the church, and got into the car. Ironically, Tommy sent me a text message at that very moment: he wanted to stay after school for a meeting. I thanked God for His clear signal, picked Allison up from the high school, and drove to the police station. During the ten-minute drive, I told Allison about the envelope's arrival.

I remember Allison quietly crying when I told her we were going to the police station—but I don't remember her resisting. No bargaining, no explanations of who the envelope's sender was, no comment about what might be in the envelope. Just quiet tears running down Allison's face as I turned the car off in the parking lot, followed by a request to stay in the car long enough so she could re-apply her mascara, eyeliner, and lip gloss before going into the police station.

Walking into the station again was nerve-wracking. Too many memories from 2009 flooded my brain, but I kept reminding myself how well that turned out.

First I had to fill out a sheet of paper saying why we were there. My hands shook while I filled out the five-and-one-half by eight-and-one-half-inch piece of paper, and I forced myself to look the clerk in the eye when I slid the paper back through the slot under the bullet-proof glass between us.

A young officer came into the lobby and led us to an interior interview room to talk. Consulting the piece of paper I filled out, he asked me, then Allison, a few questions to clarify what I had written on the paper. As we talked, he added notes to the paper. When Allison finished, he excused himself.

The young officer returned a minute or so later, followed by a plain-clothes Investigator.

The investigator introduced himself, shook hands with me, and sat in the chair directly across the table from Allison. The young officer stood quietly between the investigator and the door leading into the hall.

Allison told her story again. When she finished, the investigator carefully tore off an edge of the envelope, pushed gently on the top and bottom of the envelope to create an opening, and looked inside. Then he turned the envelope so the opening faced the tabletop, and the contents slid out.

Four sets of eyes looked at the folded white piece of paper on the table.

Four sets of eyes watched the investigator push the folded piece of paper with his pen.

Four sets of eyes witnessed the flash of green as the investigator gently pushed the white piece of paper open with the back of his pen.

The investigator sat back in his chair, his eyebrows flicked upwards, and his head turned so he could exchange a look with the young officer standing to his right in the small interview room.

After what felt like an eternity, the investigator opened the white piece of paper fully. It contained no markings of any kind—but nestled inside I saw folded American dollar bills.

I don't know the exact amount, but after a moment, the investigator picked the money up, and started unfolding it. Twenty dollar bills—three, perhaps four, from what I saw.

Now the investigator's questioning took on an edge.

Q: Why would this man be sending you money, Allison?

A: He always sends me stuff after I send him pictures.

Q: Did he ask for the pictures?

A: Yes.

Q: How many have you sent him?

A: I don't remember.

Q: And how many pictures has he sent you?

A: A lot.

Q: Does he know how old you are?

A: Yes.

Q: Do you know how old he is?

A: I think he's in his twenties. Maybe twenty-four? I don't remember.

I was re-living the nightmare of 2009—but this policeman wasn't as nice as Officer Richards had been.

Q: What else has he sent you?

A: A gift card, and that box, Mom.

That box. The mystery box that came in the mail in May 2010.

I SPOTTED THE LARGE white box between the screen door and front door when we pulled into the driveway after school, but Allison jumped out of the car as soon as I pulled the car into the garage. Before I had time to turn the car's engine off, Allison was in the house.

The house was quiet when I entered. Too quiet. "Allison, where are you?"

Silence.

I walked over to the front door, opened it, but the box was gone. "Allison?"

Silence.

I walked to my bedroom, to set my things down, then proceeded down the stairs to Allison's room. Before I got halfway down the stairs, though, Allison appeared at the bottom of the stairs, smiling, and a bit out of breath.

"Where's the box?" I asked.

"Oh, it was for me," she said.

"Oh? What is it?"

"I don't know."

"What do you mean you don't know? Who is it from?"

I expected Allison to say it was from her father, but her "I don't know" response made me uncomfortable.

"Let me see it."

"It's for me, Mom!"

"Why can't I just see it, dear?"

"Because it's for me!" Allison yelled, then turned on her heels and ran to her bedroom. When she slammed the door shut in my face, I knew there was a real problem with the box.

The next several hours passed with my yelling at Allison to unlock either the bedroom or bathroom door and show me the dumb box, Allison screaming about the box being for her which meant it was none of my business, and extended periods of silence while we waited each other out.

Finally, Allison threw an empty white post office box up the stairs. I walked down to ask her what had been inside the box, and she coquettishly produced an empty box with illustrations of vibrators on the outside—feeding me a wild story about how her friend Erin sent the box to our house. "She needs to replace her mom's vibrator, because she accidentally threw it away, and her mom would totally freak out if she knew."

Q: Whose computer have you been using to send these pictures?

A: Different computers. My friend's, mostly.

Q: Well, we're going to need the name of that friend, because we need the computer. Those pictures are stored on the computer's hard-drive, and we need to get them off. It's a crime to have those kinds of pictures because you are underage. What's the name of the friend whose computer you have been using?

The way Allison fished around for a name, I realized she was trying to protect someone. A little too late, I figured out who she was trying to protect. "Allison, have you been doing this on my work computer?"

"Yes, Mom. I'm really sorry, but it's the only computer that would work. The computer at the library won't let me download pictures from my digital camera, and . . ."

My work computer. In addition to whatever my daughter was doing to herself, she could have gotten me fired, too. What if I had accidentally opened the wrong file while teaching a class? The way the classrooms are set up, my students see the images on the screen in the front of the classroom before I do.

"Ma'am, we're going to need that computer."

I wanted to die. I wanted to kill Allison. I wanted to wake up from the nightmare I was suddenly living.

The young officer followed Allison and me in our car as we first drove over to the high school to pick up Tommy, then to our house—to get my work computer. I walked into the house, got the laptop, and brought it out to the policeman in my driveway. I provided the passwords. I gave him the cord to plug the computer into the wall outlet. I signed the form documenting the confiscation of the aforementioned property. Then the officer told me he had to take my daughter as well.

"What! She has a choir concert tonight! My mother is coming!" I couldn't understand why he wanted to take Allison. We volunteered the information in the first place, and then cooperated with everything else asked of us! Why did the police have to take Allison as well? In the interview room back at the station, the investigator *told* Allison she wasn't in trouble. Why was the young police officer taking it all back? I wanted to scream. I wanted to push him back towards his police car, run into the house, and slam the door in his face. I wanted to keep Allison safe—with me.

I'm a bright, law-abiding woman, though, and I knew I couldn't do any of those things. I had to remain calm, for Allison's sake. I had to cooperate and stay focused, for Tommy's sake. I had to let Allison's game play itself out.

When I walked back into the house, I watched Allison's face go from mild excitement ("Do we get to go to Burger King now?"), to questioning, to anxious; the officer had followed me into the house.

I walked over to Allison, wrapped her in a tight, loving hug. I tried to explain. "I'm so sorry, dear . . ." was all I could get out before she started screaming—and then slumped from my arms to the kitchen floor.

Thankfully, the police officer stood quietly in our kitchen, leaning against the kitchen counter strip that runs in front of the sink, while Allison calmed down.

"Everything will be all right," I kept repeating over and over. "God will take care of us, sweetie, just like He took care of us before."

"I love you, Mommy," Allison said as we hugged in the kitchen before she left.

"I love you too, sweetie. We'll get through this. You'll be fine."

But, how *will we get through this?* How *will we be fine?*

Once again, my lovely daughter was going into strange places without me. She was taking us places no parent ever wanted to see their child, places where I couldn't protect her.

Had I *ever* been successful in my efforts to protect her?

Where did I go wrong, as a parent?

Allison quietly followed the police officer from our house to his squad car and dutifully got into the back seat. I stood in the open garage until the police car was out of sight. Then I walked back into the house, and tried to pick up the pieces of my life once again.

My mother and I sat through the choir concert, not talking. I tried to enjoy it, for Tommy's sake (he was in the Freshman choir), but nearly cried when Allison's choir group walked onto the stage.

For once, I was glad I wasn't friends with any of the other parents. It freed me from having to explain Allison's absence.

At the same time, I wished I had someone to talk to. I wished I had someone who could hold me, someone who could tell me it wasn't my fault; someone who would love me without judging me.

A piece of me died that night—and I silently carried the pain.

Two

Juvy

ALLISON WAS REMOVED from our home sometime between four and five the afternoon of February 28, 2011. The officer took her from our house, drove directly to the juvenile facility in town (a ten-minute drive), and walked Allison in.

By ten-fifteen at night, I had endured the choir concert in smoldering silence, and just wanted Tommy and my mother to go to sleep so I could pace the house in silent darkness. Tommy was too ramped up with adrenaline, though, and headed downstairs to play a song on the piano for his grandmother. My mother got up from my spot at the dining room table, with the intention of getting ready for bed, when the phone rang. I saw the detention center's name appear on the caller ID on the home phone, and immediately wanted to silence the phone. My mother was standing two feet away from me. Had she seen the name on the caller ID as well?

I took a deep breath, picked up the phone, and said, "Hello?"

"Hi. I just want to let you know your daughter is here, and will be assessed . . ." the voice on the line began.

I remember writing down what I thought was important during the phone call, but mostly I just stared at my mother who was standing in my dining room. I was so ashamed and horrified by everything taking place. I wanted Allison home, getting ready for bed after the evening's choir concert like Tommy was doing. At the very least, I wished my mother wasn't standing in the house, witnessing my family's shame.

"So if you want to supply her with postage stamps," the voice on the phone continued, "she can write to you after her first week."

"Uhm, excuse me, what do you mean her first week? I was told she was only going to be there overnight."

"I'm sorry, ma'am, but I don't have that information. I only do the intake portion. Your daughter will be seen in juvenile court tomorrow, and the judge will decide what happens after that."

Court. Allison was going to be seen in juvenile court. I heard, I memorized, but I couldn't comprehend.

"Do you have any questions of me, then, ma'am?" the voice on the phone asked, bringing me out of my fog.

"Questions? Tons . . ." I stumbled. "But no, really, I don't. Thank you."

How could I ask any of the questions rushing through my brain, when my mother was staring at me while I listened and took notes? *What do you mean she can write to me after a week? Can I come visit her within that time? How long until I can bring her back home? What is it she has done, exactly, that allows you to take her from me and store her in* your *facility? What is she going to court for? Is that something I can show up for? What number can I call tomorrow, after my mom leaves, when I'm more able to talk freely?*

"Would you like to go to the court proceeding tomorrow, ma'am?"

"Yes. Yes, of course I would."

"Okay, then someone will call you in the morning with the time and everything."

As I returned the phone to its cradle, I wanted to simply slump into the nearest chair and stare at the wall while I absorbed everything I had heard—but my mother wouldn't let me. Like a lion sensing the weakest member of the herd, my mother pounced.

"Who was that? What was it all about?"

I mumbled something or other in the hopes of getting her to leave me alone, and then practically ran for the basement to hug Tommy.

"What's wrong, Mom?"

"Nothing. You did a really nice job tonight, honey, but you just need to go to bed now," I said in answer to his question about the unsolicited hug. "C'mon. Grandma needs to go to bed, but she won't until you do. And I have a lot of stuff to do tomorrow morning."

I really just wanted to go to bed and cry, but it would be a while before I could do either.

AFTER ALLISON WAS RELEASED from the juvenile detention center, and was back home with me, she talked about her time in juvy almost like one describing a weekend camping trip or a week-long stay at a summer camp. She told me about the clothes she wore, the food she ate, the room she slept in and the kids she met.

> When we first got there [about 5:00 p.m.], the intakes got a bag lunch. I didn't look in my bag, but the other girls had like an apple, some chips, if you could even call them chips, and a ham sandwich with little mayonnaise packets. Nothing to drink.
>
> During intake, they make you go into a shower and take off all your clothes and jewelry. They go through all of your clothes, to make sure you don't have anything, weapon wise.
>
> Then they make you stand on the other side of a metal bar, against the door, naked. They would use a metal detector, and make you hold your hands up above the door; they would make you lift up one foot at a time.
>
> After they used the metal detector, they would make you take a shower, and scrub up with the generic hand soap you find in schools—the kind that makes me itch and break out—so I didn't use it. That's your shampoo as well.
>
> They give you a really small thing of deodorant, like travel size deodorant. They give you a comb, too, and a small, small towel, like a hand towel. You can shower once a day, at their designated time in the morning. Probably around 5:30 a.m.; we weren't allowed to look at clocks.
>
> The water was as cold as ice. They made you shower for about five minutes total, non stop. Then they would throw your state-issued clothes over the door, and make you wear other people's underwear.

Orange socks, white underwear, two white shirts that you had to wear at all times, a bright orange, huge sweater, and dark-blue guys' sweatpants that you can't roll up, no matter how big they are. You were sometimes allowed to wear your own bra—I was. You were allowed two hair ties, but they can't be on your wrists. You had to change into shorts for bed.

To be able to wear your own socks and underwear, you have to earn them back with good behavior and volunteering. So if you're talking after lights out, you lose that privilege for another day or two.

After that, I think you would be able to wear your own shirt, and possibly pants and sweater, but it takes a couple of days, possibly more than a week, to earn your shoes back—and you have to do a lot of volunteering, and earn a lot of points. You always had to wear socks, though; my feet were freezing.

First, I was given XL pants. Ten minutes later, after telling them that they were way too big to even keep up, I was given a pair of L pants. They wouldn't stay up either, so I rolled them up; I didn't tell them, though. The crotch was still down to my knees, and the bottoms of the pants went over my feet—so I had to hold them up like a dress when I walked. (Reason I fell during basketball—and why the teacher thought I didn't have socks on. No one could see my feet . . .)

My roommate had her own clothes; her own deodorant and shampoo. I don't know about her own shoes . . .

She taught me how to make my own bed.

After that, they make you sit in the other room, and interview you about any and all information.

After that, you get issued your room . . .

When you go into your room, you get a cup, a little tiny cup, and you can drink from the sink—when given permission.

I felt like an animal locked in a cage. I didn't understand why I had to be there; why I had to shower on command, why I had to have the lights out at 9:00 p.m., and get up at 5:00 in the morning.

Breakfast was at around 6:00 in the morning. Breakfast was a sausage patty and two tiny square waffles that weren't even eggo brand [maybe two inches by two inches], and orange juice.

After breakfast but before school, we were allowed to brush our teeth. The toothpaste tasted like paste, with a tiny hint of mint.

[Allison would later describe it as being the consistency of "the stuff they put between the concrete blocks, with a little bit of mint added in."] The mint lasts a minute; the other flavor lasts hours.

We had "school" in juvy. We had to line up in the boy's section, in a line.

The fifteen-year-old I met, and had classes together with . . .

We went to English first, and had to take a reading assessment quiz. After we took that, the teacher told us how well we read, and we had to go over to the mini bookshelves and pick out a book. I chose one about a girl who was in the Holocaust. She was a German, and somehow died and became a Jew. I don't know.

Then we got the opportunity to write, but we had to turn everything in. I wrote about my many eating disorders, and why my self-consciousness is so high? If that makes sense. Why I'm so self-conscious.

Then we had to go to science. It wasn't science. We watched a movie about antelopes having sex.

Then we went to math, and wa—

No, we went to social studies. Social studies was when we watched the stuff about the antelope. After we went to social studies, we went to science, and watched the movie *Stargate*.

Then I think we went to math. And math we watched, I don't even know what we watched, it was stupid.

Then we went to gym, and the girl and I were on one side of the gym and the guys were on the other. We had to constantly shoot baskets. We couldn't stop for more than thirty seconds, or we would get yelled at. Unfortunately, we weren't allowed to wear shoes, and so I fell when I was running after the basketball.

The teacher asked me why I fell. He asked if I was even wearing socks.

After that, we went to lunch. Nasty chilly and sandwiches without anything. Turkey sandwiches on bread, and gross chili with crackers. I didn't eat.

After that, we went to what they call "elective," which my class was going to learn about juvenile discipline judiciary stuff. I got called out to talk to my court appointed lawyer.

When I got back, I had to go to reading, which was just reading. You got to read the book you had chosen. I got called out, though, to go to court. [Court time of 1:30 p.m.]

> During science or math, one of my male teachers called a pizza place and ordered pizza, bread sticks, and Diet Pepsi or whatever. Then, during lunch, it got brought to him. He sat there and was talking about how good the pizza was. After everyone was done eating, he mumbled something to a table, and one of the girls got up and grabbed half of a bread stick.
>
> After a few more people did it, I learned he was having the people at the tables play rock-paper-scissors, and whoever won got half a breadstick. I didn't want anything, so I just automatically let the girl at my table have it. We're not allowed to talk across, table to table, either, and if two people were brought in together, from the same crime, you weren't allowed to talk together at all, even in the lunch line. So, if you were brought in together, if one's in the lunch line, the other has to sit at a table until the first one is sitting down.

Listening to Allison describe her time in the juvenile detention center was really, really hard. Part of the difficulty, though, was her matter-of-fact descriptions. It was almost as if being in there didn't bother her at all.

On the other hand, was any of her tale true? Over the years, I've come to realize much of what Allison says, or sends in a text message, or posts to her social networking site is borrowed. She reads a lot of fiction about troubled teenagers, she watches a lot of reality TV, she copies a lot of sayings from websites on the Internet. Can I trust the details she describes, or did she borrow them from some book she read? The day she came home from the juvenile detention center, and told me the details I typed into the computer, I was still willing to believe—and trust—everything she said.

In my younger days, I told people I would do *anything* to protect my children. Listening to Allison's description of juvy, I began to wonder if my mother-love could extend to doing something that might land me in jail.

THREE

COURT

TUESDAY MORNING. I herded my mother out of the house while yelling for Tommy to get into the car. Although my mother offered to take Tommy to school, and then return to stay with me at the house, I really just wanted to be alone. I was too ashamed to have an audience, too ashamed to have my mother see me not handling my own family as well as people give her credit for handling *hers*. I know it sounds awful, but I don't give my mom full credit for the way I turned out. My fears should also get substantial credit for keeping me on the straight and narrow.

Finally, minutes after eleven, the phone rang.

"I'm just letting you know your daughter will be seen in court today at 1:00 p.m. Are you planning on being there?" the voice on the phone asked.

"Yes," I replied.

"Okay. Her court appointed attorney isn't able to be there today, but someone else from their office will be there with your daughter."

Allison's court-appointed attorney. I wondered what she needed an attorney for but didn't ask. I had to gather my things and get to the courthouse.

I was back in the same courthouse Allison and I last entered in 2010, when she and I were both subpoenaed to testify against the father who helped her run away in 2009. Although the building only had four floors, all visitors were limited to riding in the elevator. Personnel who worked in the building were allowed to use locked staircases to travel from one floor to the next, but security concerns limited access within the building. I hate elevators but dutifully rode it to the second floor, and stepped out into the interior hallway.

There are two courtrooms on the second floor, one on either side of the elevator doors. Not knowing which Allison's case was assigned to, I stood out in the hallway, then sat on a bench, checking my watch every minute or so. As it got closer to one o'clock, other people got off the elevator and drifted around in the hallway, but none of them were Allison. When everyone else in the hallway disappeared, though, and the hallway was empty again except for me, I got nervous. My watch said it was 1:15 p.m.

Just before I reached complete panic mode, the left courtroom door opened up, and a man stuck his head out. "Are you Allison's mom?"

"Yes."

"She's going to be in here. I'm . . ."

I didn't care who he was—I just wanted to see my daughter. But I was an adult, and I knew enough to honor the gesture of his outstretched arm. We shook hands, then he motioned for me to enter the courtroom through the next set of doors.

As I entered from the back doors, Allison was brought in through an interior side door. She was wearing ankle shackles over her winter boots. I nearly collapsed on the courtroom floor at the sight, but made it to the corner of the last bench and sat down.

Allison's attorney motioned for her to sit on the bench to his right, then signaled for me to come closer, to join Allison as it were. I sat on the bench directly behind her.

It was March 1, 2011, and I was watching my seventeen-year-old daughter being arraigned on felony charges: Dissemination of Child Pornography. It didn't make sense to me, because I only thought she emailed a topless picture of herself to someone, but she spent the past twenty-one hours in the juvenile detention center in town while I paced the floors at home, not eating, and not sleeping.

We all stood as the judge entered the room, and I immediately recognized him. He was the same judge who presided over the case I was called to jury duty for, the day after my first experience in court with Allison in 2010. Fortunately, I was dismissed from jury duty very quickly. I hoped he didn't remember me, or why I was dismissed.

"So, what brings us here today?" the judge began.

The young, female county attorney stood up to present her case. "I haven't had time to review everything yet," she explained, "because the defendant has quite a history." As she said this, she held up two file folders full of papers. "All I know at this time, your honor, is that the defendant confessed yesterday to sending nude pictures, via the Internet."

I watched the county attorney continue grand-standing, making Allison out to be the worst criminal in the state, based on the five inches of paper held within the two file folders. Five inches of paper, all documenting the investigation—and subsequent court cases—resulting from Allison's running away from home in 2009. I didn't know this at the time, but Allison's court-appointed public defender explained it all to me when she showed me her matching set of files during our first meeting a week later.

The grand-standing efforts of the county attorney worked, though. Since no one in the courtroom but Allison knew the entire truth of what she did, the judge granted the motion to postpone the case until all parties had a chance to review the evidence.

Before we were excused for the day, Allison's public-defender-for-the-day requested house arrest while Allison waited for a later review of the case, rather than a return to the juvenile detention center. Considering Allison was still attending high school, he argued, and her grades were all solidly good, the public defender felt it would be in Allison's best interest to go home. "Her mother is even here, your Honor," the public defender said, motioning to me directly behind Allison.

Without comprehending what was at stake, I was asked to stand and speak on Allison's behalf.

"Is this true, ma'am?" the judge asked.

The public defender motioned for me to speak into the microphone attached to the table, but I didn't want to bend awkwardly over the bench in front of me, nor take the time to trust my knees to carry me calmly and carefully around the bench to stand in front of the table. I spoke to lecture hall rooms of students every day without a microphone. I was confident in my voice's ability to carry the ten feet to the judge's bench in front of the nearly empty courtroom. "Yes," I began, my voice shaking with adrenaline. "Allison is taking a couple college classes through the high school, and we in fact have parent-teacher conferences tonight."

"Who else lives in the home with you?" the judge enquired.

"Just Allison, her younger brother, Tommy, and me."

"And you're okay with this arrangement the public defender is requesting?"

"Yes."

"Okay, thank you. You may sit back down."

I gently touched Allison's left shoulder with my right hand on the way back down, and re-focused my attention on slowing the beat of my racing heart.

"I'm placing you on house arrest, Allison," the judge began, "which means your mother is in charge. Do you understand me? You have to do everything your mother tells you, or else you are going to go back to juvy.

"You can go to school, but must go directly to school in the morning, and go directly home after school.

"You cannot leave the house," the judge continued, "without your mother.

"You also cannot use the Internet without your mother, or a school teacher over twenty-one years of age next to you.

"You also can't use a digital camera, an iPod, any cell phones other than to call 911, or any other electronic equipment that can transmit pictures."

"But sir," I wanted to say, *"her iPod is such an old model it doesn't have a camera, or transmitter capability. And, I disconnected her ability to send or receive pictures with her cell phone two years ago, when I discovered there was a fee for every second of data-use used. You can check with our cell phone provider, if you don't believe me."* All the things I wanted to say, but no one gave me a chance.

"And finally," the judge continued, "you cannot contact any of the people mentioned to the police yesterday, when they were questioning you. That includes Daniel."

Allison screamed, then burst into hysterical tears while sitting in her chair at the defendant's table. Daniel was Allison's boyfriend. They had been dating for nine months.

"Allison, I need you to hear me about these rules. You are facing some really serious charges here, and I'm sending you home rather than sending you back to the detention center."

Allison's gray-haired male public defender turned and harshly whispered at her to "Shut up, now. You're getting to go home . . ." while I shoved her face into the side of my coat to muffle her cries. Through it all, I kept nodding to the judge while he spoke to Allison. I kept rubbing Allison's back to get her to quiet down like I did during toddler-era temper-tantrums. I kept quietly "shhh"ing her and whispering, "It will be okay" in a soothing voice, hoping to calm her down.

Allison's ankle-shackles were removed, and we left the court room together. In alternating waves, I was happy, relieved, and tired.

"Where's the bathroom?" Allison asked as soon as we stepped into the hallway.

I saw the sign further down the hall, pointed it out, and followed Allison into the small room with one sink, and one stall. Allison headed directly to the sink, rather than the stall, and asked me for the bag someone had handed me along the way.

Ah, yes, her jewelry.

Two sets of piercings in each ear had morphed into a set of gauges and a regular set of earring holes. She also had a nose ring, a lip piercing, and an eyebrow piercing.

Once the jewelry was back in place, Allison headed into the stall to urinate. Then she asked about the Burger King stop she was denied twenty-two hours earlier.

Really, dear? That's all you care about—and in that order? Piercings, Burger King, and then television shows when we get home? How about an explanation? Or at the very least, an apology to your mom? Is that too much to ask?

Four

House Arrest

No sooner had we gotten home, than Allison began expressing her concerns about Daniel. "Mom, I have to call Daniel and let him know what's going on. He's going to think I'm breaking up with him or something. We haven't talked since you picked me up from school yesterday. Can I please just have my cell phone for that? Please?"

I was angry Allison was more concerned about Daniel's feelings than she seemed to be about mine. But, she'd heard me tell her my love is unconditional about a million times. Had she ever heard the same from Daniel?

"If you just give me my phone," Allison's bargaining began, "I'll just call him and tell him I'm all right, and . . ."

"No, dear. You heard the judge. Letting you call Daniel on your cell phone would be two violations, right off the top. If they find out about it, you'll be back in juvy before you can even ask why."

"But how will they find out about it, Mom?"

"I don't know, dear. I don't know how this works. Are they going to check your cell phone usage? I don't know. But, they might speak with Daniel, as part of the investigation. Would he be able to lie, and tell them he's had no contact with you at all? I don't want to do anything to risk losing you again."

"But I've got to tell him, Mom. He's probably already freaking out because we haven't talked for two days."

As an adult, it's difficult to imagine what is so traumatic about not talking to each other for two days. But, these are kids, kids who have cell phones that can send pictures as well as text messages, kids who communicate with each other more times in a day than I communicate with some friends or family in a month. For these kids, two days of not talking might signal a death—or a break-up.

I decided on a compromise. I would call Daniel on my cell phone. I put the call on speaker, so Allison could hear everything Daniel said first-hand, but Allison was not allowed to speak to Daniel. Instead, Allison whispered her responses to me, and I relayed the messages to Daniel.

"Hi, Daniel," I began. "Allison is fine, but she's in some trouble with the police and can't talk to you while they do some investigation work."

"What do you mean she's in trouble?" Daniel interrupted. "What kind of trouble?"

"I can't really tell you anything about it, Daniel, because they might want to talk to you as well."

"Talk to me? About what?"

"Allison sent some pictures of herself over the Internet."

"I still don't understand. What's wrong with that?"

"That's really all I can tell you right now, Daniel. At some point, Allison will be able to explain it all to you herself, just not right now."

"Well, can I talk to her?"

"Not right now, Daniel. Your name came up when she was talking about stuff with the police, so the conditions of her house arrest include not talking to you."

"What do you mean?"

"Allison is here, with me, but she's on house arrest. She can't use her iPod, her digital camera, the Internet, or her cell phone until they tell her differently. The judge let her come home because she's in school, and doing well academically, so he doesn't want to disrupt that. But, she can only go to school. The rest of the time she has to be with me."

"Wow."

"Yep. But, we're happy she can at least be home."

"How long will this take?"

"I have no idea. We have another court date scheduled for next week, so hopefully we'll know something more by then."

"You mean I can't talk to Allison for a week?"

"That's right. Not until the judge says it's okay again. But, she'll call you again as soon as she can."

From that point, the conversation got mushy. Allison wanted me to reassure Daniel she still loved him, and would stay faithful to him. Daniel reciprocated in kind.

A week later, a similar telephone conversation took place. "Sorry, Daniel, there is no change. Allison's public defender asked the judge if the limitation on you could be lifted, but the judge said no."

"Why?"

"I don't know, Daniel. You're part of the investigation, and they aren't done with it yet. So, we have to wait, and go back in two weeks."

"Two weeks!"

"I know. Allison and I feel the same way. But she says she loves you . . ."

STANDING IN THE COURT room on March 1st, I told the judge about Allison's doing so well in school—and mentioned having conferences. After she ate her Burger King lunch, listened to the phone call to Daniel, and took a shower, Allison happily accompanied me to parent-teacher conferences.

The first thing I noticed when we got to the high school was Allison's attitude change—bravado replaced sullenness. "Yeah," she told kids who approached, "I can't text you because I'm on house arrest. I was in juvy yesterday and today. I've got to stick with my mom, now."

I was embarrassed by the past twenty-four hours, but Allison was using it to gain more attention from classmates.

Talking with the teachers got even more awkward.

"Well, *this* is odd!" they each said in their turn. "I can't find her in my [computerized] grade-book. I just printed the master list this afternoon, in preparation for conferences. I don't understand why she's not on here!"

By the time the third teacher echoed the confusion expressed by the first and second teacher, I decided the school had an automatic updating system in conjunction with the detention center. Part of the intake process, perhaps, converted children from the rolls of the high school to the rolls of the juvenile detention center for state accountability purposes.

Does everyone get to know—and judge?

EIGHTEEN DAYS AFTER ALLISON and I walked out of the court room together, I started to realize the level of punishment house arrest can be. My friend Sara sent me a text in the afternoon, saying "I think this should be called Mom arrest instead of house arrest."

I sent back a text message saying "Yep—or how-to-torture-the-single-mom-to-the-point-of-submission arrest."

The problem became the level of Allison's anxiety. On March 1st, the judge took away three of Allison's limbs: her iPod (a seventeen-year-old without her favorite music), her cell phone (teenagers don't talk on phones anymore, they send text messages—which a house phone cannot do), and her eighteen-year-old boyfriend of nine months. Much like a toddler without his favorite binky, or a frightened child who is told she can no longer have her favorite stuffed animal at night, Allison struggled with the nightmare her life became. Instead of soldiering through, like I had to do, she reverted to the child she once was, and began sleeping with me (king-size bed) the night she came home from juvy.

Daylight hours weren't much better, unfortunately. Allison told me she was afraid to stay home alone, for fear the police would return—and take her from our home like they did the afternoon of February 28th.

By March 2nd, Allison was my shadow. When not in school, Allison was with me. In the house, Allison followed me from room to room. Running to the store for an item or two, taking Tommy to his piano lesson, going to bed at night—Allison was with me. She even wanted to join me for my three-month periodontal cleaning with the dentist, but I assured her she would be fine, at home, with her fifteen-year-old brother for the hour I would be sitting in the dental chair.

Leaving the courtroom on March 1st, we hoped the restrictions would only be short-term. Allison's next court appearance was scheduled for the following week.

March 8th. I walked towards the court house with Allison next to me, unlike the week before, but nearly froze in place on the sidewalk as I approached the glass doors. Officer Vic Richards was in charge of courthouse security screening for the day. Although I had thought about him a million times since we met on Saturday, April 25th, 2009, I hadn't seen or spoken to him since I received the letter from the police chief in June of 2009, telling me to "cease and desist" after sending Vic a note of thanks and two boxes of Girl Scout cookies I thought he could share with the other staff in the lunch room. Knowing I was entering the courthouse because Allison was in trouble again was just too embarrassing. I wanted to run away and hide my shame in private somewhere.

Sadly, I realized there was no way to avoid Officer Richards. There was no alternate entrance Allison and I could use. There was no way to re-schedule for another day, when he wouldn't be working. There was no way for me to slip past him, sight unseen.

Allison entered the building in front of me, and I noticed Officer Richards stand up when I walked through the second glass door. I couldn't force my eyes to meet his, though. Head down, I fumbled with my purse, mittens, and notepad, placing them on the conveyor belt between Officer Richards and me while Allison proceeded through the arch of the metal detector. Allison didn't see my hands shaking horribly. She didn't acknowledge Officer Richards with a greeting of familiarity.

When we were safely in the elevator, alone, and the doors closed, I released the strangle-hold on my emotions. "Oh, my, oh, my, oh, my. Did you see who that was?"

"No," came Allison's indifferent response.

"It was Officer Richards!"

"Oh! Why didn't you say something to him? He looked like he wanted to say something to you, Mom."

I have wanted to say something to Vic Richards for nearly two years. I've wanted to thank him for his help with Allison, to tell him how I appreciated his non-judgmental handling of our case in 2009, to ask him if I can buy him a cup of coffee, to ask him if he really meant it when he said I was "an amazing woman" the day we were alone, in the doorway of the police station, while Allison took a bathroom break after testifying about the predator who sent her the bus tickets to run away from home.

But the shame of being back in the courthouse with Allison had become too much for me. Since 2009, I've constantly felt like I'm a failure as a mother, rather than an amazing woman. I can't imagine someone with Vic Richards' job ever being interested in a woman like me, a woman who can't keep her teenage daughter on the straight-and-narrow.

By the time the elevator doors opened on the second floor, I was once again composed and focused on Allison. I was preparing myself for what we were about to face.

This time, a female judge was presiding. Allison's public defender explained how she hadn't had a chance to review the images from the computer yet. "We would like to re-visit one of the restrictions, though, if we could," Allison's public defender continued.

"We would like to lift the restriction of having no contact with Daniel, Allison's eighteen-year-old boyfriend."

The judge let Allison's attorney voice the request. She allowed me to provide my position on the request, as well as explain the influence Daniel was having in Allison's life. Sadly, the judge denied the request to lift the restriction. "The matter is still under investigation . . ."

Allison's tears were quieter this time, thankfully. I warned her about keeping the sound out of the outburst before we left the car. This time, she only sniffled while the tears streamed down her face.

The judge scheduled Allison's next court appearance for March 29th, then called a court officer forward. Allison had never been officially "Booked" (fingerprinted) for the crime. We had to do that before we could leave the building.

Walking out of the building in plain view of Vic Richards again was hard. I wanted to stop and talk to him. I wanted to turn and at least smile. But, I had just witnessed my seventeen-year-old daughter get finger-printed. I couldn't imagine anyone being romantically interested in the mother of a felon.

March 29th passed, as did several other court dates. The public defender kept postponing the case because there was no news on the computer analysis, nor any images for the public defender to view.

Publicly, Allison and I tried to continue with a "normal" teenage life. At 7:50am Saturday, April 9th, I dropped Allison off to take her A.C.T. test. Sunday, after church, I drove the kids and one of Allison's new girl friends to a mall 150 miles east of our home. As we prepared for bed that night, Allison said, "Today was the greatest day. I've never had so much fun shopping with a friend before! She even let me go to stores that I wanted to." When Allison's grade report for third term arrived in the home mailbox, I was thrilled to see two "A"s and two "B"s, in spite of all the stress.

Our next court date was scheduled for Thursday, April14th. I was nervous. I was sure Allison was nervous too, but there was nothing I could do or say to ease it. Monday night, the 11th, Allison broke. "I hope it's just all over Thursday. Give me a misdemeanor, tell me what my punishment is, but just let me talk to Daniel."

I didn't know what to say anymore. I wanted my bed back, my freedom back, my life back. But, how exactly would my life change after Thursday's court date?

If Allison were to be convicted of a felony . . .

If Allison were to be charged with a misdemeanor . . .

If Allison were to be released . . . I would get my bed back, she would return to her basement room where she talks to Daniel on the phone for hours at a time—but would Allison's behavior change?

April 12th. We had been on house arrest since March 1st. Day forty-three, Allison was still sleeping with me, she still couldn't talk to her boyfriend Daniel, and she was swinging on her swing whenever the weather was clear.

Two weekends before, we drove to the zoo two hundred miles to the south, celebrating the first fifty-degree weekend of the season. It was hard for Allison, being only fifty miles from Daniel's home, and not being able to see him or speak with him. She tried negotiating an "accidental" meeting with him at the zoo, which I wanted to grant—but I know I'm a bad liar. "What if we go back to court, dear, and they point blank ask me if you have had any contact with Daniel since February 28th? I won't be able to pull it off."

Allison cried herself to sleep that night.

I also wanted to cry, but couldn't. My dad trained me not to cry.

I constantly felt so empty, but then felt guilty about my own emptiness. It wasn't like I had been diagnosed with cancer, my brain scolded, or like I'd lost someone close. All I had essentially lost was my freedom, and my peace of mind.

So much pain inside, so much shame.

I remember my sister always cried when we were young. My mother might have too, but I don't remember. I remember my sister crying.

My sister, three and a half years older than I, naturally became my role model for a lot of things. When my sister cried, my dad yelled.

"You better stop crying," he'd yell, "or I'll *give* you something to cry about."

I thought he didn't like her crying because her face got all scrunched up when she cried.

I learned not to cry because my sister's crying made my dad's yelling get worse.

I remember crying when a boy I liked at sixteen didn't like me back. I remember being at a party or something with my best friend Hans, and then hiding in a dark corner in the basement of the house so I could cry. I felt ugly, crying—liquid streaming down my face, leaving black trails of mascara and eyeliner, liquid streaming from my nose, nearly running into my mouth.

At forty-eight, I made a conscious decision to start trying to give myself permission to cry.

FINALLY, THE CALL WE had been waiting for. According to the phone's caller ID register, the public defender called at 2:31 p.m., but no one was home. Allison was the first to see the caller ID when we got home from school.

"Hi, Jeanette. Give me a call back," the public defender's voice said from the answering machine. No indication of what our conversation would cover, just a request to call her back.

By 4:00 p.m., I finally heard the words Allison and I had been waiting over forty days to hear: "The charges are being dismissed."

I wanted to collapse with relief into the nearest chair, but the public defender wasn't done.

"I haven't seen the actual paperwork, yet," she continued, "so, Allison still shouldn't have any contact with Daniel or anything until I get the document in my hand."

Yikes.

"I'll give you a call as soon as I have it, but it might not be until tomorrow."

The seventeen-year-old child was free, but she still couldn't have her cell phone, her iPod, her camera, unsupervised Internet access, or contact with her boyfriend until a piece of paper made its way from the prosecuting attorney's office on the fourth floor of the courthouse to the public defender's office—across the street.

Allison and I waited. We waited because it was important for me to do the right thing.

Twenty-four hours after she told me the charges were being dismissed, I called the public defender's office again. "Just checking in," I began.

"Well, I still haven't seen anything from the prosecutor's office, but we also haven't received our afternoon mail yet."

Four o'clock on a Wednesday afternoon. When would the afternoon mail arrive?

"Let me look on the computer," she said. "It shows that we are off the docket for court tomorrow. The charges are dismissed by the prosecuting side. But, this other screen still shows it as an open case."

Doing her job, the public defender advised me to wait. "Be careful," she said as though reading my mind. "And good luck," she added before we each hung up.

I didn't need luck—I needed strength, patience, and Allison's cooperation.

I also know how slowly the wheels of justice can move. On April 1, 1998, for example, I appeared in court to obtain a divorce from the children's father. Since he didn't hire an attorney, or come to court, I was divorced by "default"—but the paperwork wasn't signed by a judge until April 13, 1998. For twelve days I considered myself divorced although it wasn't official. During those twelve days, I didn't do anything that would bring my marital status into question. When I received the official document in the mail, it felt anti-climactic—and somewhat false.

Fifteen years later, I'm still using April 1st as the marker of my divorce, not April 13th.

The official document, dismissing the charges against Allison, was signed April 12th. I received a copy in the mail Friday, April 15th. According to the envelope's postmark, it was mailed on Thursday, April 14th.

WITH ALLISON CLEARED of all charges, then, the return of the computer became a priority.

Every day, I waited for the police car to pull into my driveway. Every day, I checked our home phone's answering machine for pick-up instructions. Every day, I hoped to get the laptop back. The morning of April 19th, I decided I had waited long enough. I dropped the kids off at school, then drove over to the police station with my yellow carbon-copy property receipt.

"Hi, I'd like to pick up my property," I politely said to the girl sitting behind the bullet-proof glass as I slid my property receipt under the glass.

"And you are?" she asked.

While I told her my name, she pointed down to my name written on the yellow paper, nodded, then turned to the computer on her desk.

"Have you made an appointment to pick it up?" she asked after verifying my photo identification through the computer on her desk.

"Um, no. I didn't know I had to do that."

"Yeah, they like to make an appointment so they can get it out of the property room. Let me call the investigator and see . . ." I didn't hear the rest of what she said, because she turned away from the bullet proof glass while reaching for the phone to the left of the computer.

"The investigator said he hasn't received a release form yet. You have to contact your attorney. Your attorney will contact the county attorney's office, and the county attorney's office will send a release form to the investigator."

"But the charges were dismissed."

"The county attorney's office hasn't sent over the release form, though."

"Can I just go over to the county attorney's office myself?" Considering all three of these offices are adjacent to each other, it seemed like a logical solution.

"Well, I suppose you could. But then you'll still need to make an appointment to pick it up."

Aaaaaarrrrghhhhhhhhh. I'm here, right now. Why can't I have my dumb computer back right now?

I left the building starting to boil, and walked halfway across the street to the courthouse doors before I remembered the security screening doesn't allow cell phones to enter the building. I pivoted back to the left, and walked to the car instead.

I was faced with two choices. I could either: a) Put my cell phone into the car, go through the screening at the courthouse, ride the elevator to the fourth floor, and walk over to the county attorney's office where someone will tell me the request will be passed along to the attorney herself, or b) get into my car, call the public defender from my cell phone, and drive back home to get some work done. Considering the futility of option a), I proceeded with option b).

The public defender sounded surprised when I told her all of what I was told at the police station, but cheerily said she would email the county attorney right away—even though they were going to see each other in court in an hour—so there would be a document trail.

As I drove home, I also called the investigator. In my best efforts to remain calm through my growing rage, I left a message on his machine. "I was unaware of the protocol, so I would like to now request an appointment to pick up the laptop and its extension cord. Or, do I have to wait to make the appointment until after the paperwork has been sent over? And since I have to do all of this, rather than you guys just bringing it back to the house like I thought would happen, since you got it from the house in the first place, I would also like the two phones that were taken two years ago. I have a receipt for the one cell phone and charger, but not for the second one that two officers who weren't assigned to the case took with them when they came over to the house."

Five minutes after I got home my phone rang, but I was too angry to risk picking it up.

"Yep," the investigator's message began, "that is the protocol I have to follow. As soon as I get the release form, I'll be able to get the computer back to you. However, it's still at the BCA office (250 miles away), and I don't know when it's going to get shipped back up here."

Wednesday, April 27th. I still didn't have the computer back from the police, or word on when it might be made available to me, but another piece of normality had returned. The previous night, Allison and I had one of those silly mother-daughter fights. In order to "punish" me for yelling at her, Allison walked into my bedroom, picked up her pillow and stuffed animals, and announced she was going to be sleeping in her own room for the night. Fifty-three nights after Allison's house arrest began, I got to sleep in my bed alone again.

FINALLY, THE INVESTIGATOR on the case called the house on July 1st, letting me know the computer had been returned—wiped clean of all information.

FIVE

COUNSELING, AGAIN

APRIL 19TH, SOMEONE from the Child Services office in town called the house. She told me I needed to get Allison into counseling, and asked if I had insurance to cover the expense. When I told her I already set up an appointment with a therapist, she asked me for the name of the therapist, asked when our initial appointment was scheduled for, and told me to keep in touch with her throughout the process. On the one hand, I was thrilled to discover there are safety nets in place to catch kids after they hit the courts. On the other hand, I was annoyed by the requirement I "keep in touch" with the county social worker. I wasn't a dead-beat parent, I wanted to tell her. I wasn't the one who created the behavior Allison had been exhibiting since we moved to town in 2008.

(I never spoke to anyone from the Child Services office in town again. Is this how kids fall between the cracks?)

I got tired of everyone's well-meaning advice how to help Allison, because it felt like empty words when no follow-up support was offered. The police investigator, for instance, called and asked if Allison had ever been molested—after I endured watching both the computer and my teenage daughter leave my house in police custody on February 28th.

"That's what she said," I answered matter-of-factly. "She told me about it when we lived out west."

"Did she ever see anyone about it?" the investigator asked.

"Yes, but no one did anything about it. That's part of why we moved back."

"I ask because sometimes that can cause this kind of behavior."

I knew the police investigator meant the best with his comment, but I bristled at what I felt was an attack against my parenting. He didn't know Allison. He didn't understand Allison had claimed to be sexually active long before she claimed to be molested by the boy at the library in Wyoming. He didn't understand Allison constantly seeks the attention of men. He didn't understand Allison tells stories in order to gain attention from people in general. He didn't understand the generalization he was making to a survivor of childhood sexual abuse.

He didn't understand I had given up so many personal dreams and opportunities for the sake of my children.

FRANK AND I MOVED to Minnesota in 1991. I wanted to work in advertising. I had been a copywriter for a mail-order catalog house in Chicago before we moved. I didn't have a bachelor's degree, though. None of the advertising agencies I interviewed for in Minnesota those first months would hire me.

When Frank moved out of the house in 1997, I tried to figure out how to make ends meet. I finally decided to return to college full-time. A year and a half later, I graduated with a B.A. in English.

The degree didn't solve everything, though. The new problem was I lived too far away from the advertising agencies in Minneapolis.

I also had two young children at home.

I pursued a career as a realtor next, but discovered the complexities of doing that as a single-parent of two very young children.

I'll never forget the fears of showing a house to a man by myself. I'll never forget the fear I felt the one night a male realtor asked to stop by the house after 10:00 p.m. to drop off or pick up some paperwork. I still remember the embarrassment I felt while trying to show a young couple a lovely house in the country—when my children came running through the empty house, squirting each other with the water toys they had been given in their fast-food drive-through kids' meals.

I sold one house, but without the court ordered child support payments Frank neglected to make, I quickly discovered I couldn't afford the lapses between commission checks.

My social life took a worse hit.

I had none.

ALLISON AND I MET with her third counselor in four years. Our third female counselor, our third counseling office, our third chance to get Allison's life back on track.

"Hi," the counselor greeted us in the waiting room. "My name is Mary. Why don't you both follow me."

I let Allison go first. I wanted her to be comfortable. I wanted Allison to select her chair in the office first.

Allison picked the single chair closest to the window, then pointed for me to take the chair between her and the door. Mary sat at the chair in front of her desk, forming the third leg of our triangle.

"So, tell me what brings you here today," Mary began.

Allison and I exchanged looks, waiting for the other one to speak first.

"Well, I got in trouble again," Allison finally said.

"Trouble? What do you mean by trouble, Allison?" Mary asked.

"I was charged with a felony, because they said I was distributing child pornography to a guy I met online. But the charges were dismissed, so I don't really know why I had to come."

"Tell me more about this guy you were sending pictures to."

"What do you want to know?" Allison's tone became defensive quickly, I noted.

"Well, you said you met him online. So it's not somebody you ever knew before?"

"No. Just some guy."

"So, how did you end up sending him pictures of yourself?"

"He asked for them."

"And what would he do then? Would he send you pictures of himself back?"

"Yeah, but I didn't really want them."

"So, why did you send him the pictures of yourself? Was this guy you met online sending you money for the pictures you sent?"

"He sent me stuff more than he sent money."

"Stuff? What kind of stuff, Allison?"

"Like gift cards."

"And the box, Allison. Don't forget that," I interjected.

"The box?" Mary asked.

Allison looked at the floor, then looked back up at Mary. "Yeah, he sent me a box with vibrators."

"What were you supposed to do with the vibrators, Allison?"

"What do you mean?" Allison asked with a giggle.

"Were you supposed to use them? Were you supposed to send him pictures of you using them?" Mary continued.

"Oh. Yeah," Allison replied as her eyes reverted back to the floor in front of her chair.

"Did you use them?" Mary asked. "Did you send him the pictures he wanted?"

"No. My mom totally freaked out about them even being in the house, and made me take them over to my friend Erin's house right away."

"Did Erin want them? Was she going to use the vibrators, and send pictures of herself using them to the guy?"

"I don't know. I told my mom Erin had ordered them and sent them to my house so she could replace her mom's vibrator, because I wanted my mom to stop yelling at me."

"Does your mom yell at you a lot, Allison?"

"Yeah."

"No I don't," I said in my defense.

"Yes you do, Mom."

"So tell me more about the pictures you were sending, Allison," Mary prompted, getting us back on track.

Five minutes later, Mary told me I could leave the room. She would bring Allison out when they were done.

On the way home from their first session together, Allison told me Mary gave Allison a homework assignment. "She gave me the names of two books I should look at, Mom. So, when can we go to the bookstore?"

I never asked Allison about the books. I simply took her to the bookstore the following weekend, and watched as she approached the store clerk with her list of titles.

"They have one of the books, Mom, but I have to order the other one."

"Okay."

I never saw the titles of the books until we got home but nothing could have prepared me for what they were: *Ghosts in the Bedroom: A Guide for Partners of Incest Survivors* by Ken Graber, M.A., and *Out of the Shadows: Understanding Sexual Addiction* by Patrick Carnes, Ph.D.

Once the initial shock passed, I stopped to wonder why in the world Mary would suggest Allison read either of those books. Was Allison telling Mary lies about having a sexual relationship with her father? Frank's problems weren't with sex, I didn't think—drugs were the problem. But was it possible? Then I remembered the one time, several years earlier, when Allison gave me a note saying she had some sort of memory about being in the bathtub with her father when she was little. She said he had touched her "inappropriately," but I could never ask her any questions about it, or bring up the subject in any way, shape, or form. Already knowing Allison's penchant for drama, and her tendency to tell stories as a way to gain attention, I honored her request never to ask. I honestly believed it was nonsense anyway. Frank moved out of the house before Allison celebrated her fourth birthday, and moved two states away when I filed for divorce a month after her fourth birthday. In all the years since, Frank hadn't sent child support, or cared to see the children more than the three or four times I drove them to his place for a brief visit. Even when Allison ran away from home in 2009, all Frank could do was talk about himself. While I didn't believe Frank molested Allison, I wasn't about to argue with Allison, either. I held my breath, and waited to see what Mary would uncover.

Allison read the book about sexual addiction in two days.

"Here, Mom, you have to read this book," she said when she was done. "It's very interesting."

I tried. I could only read through page thirty-six, though, before I became too sick to my stomach to read any further. I couldn't wrap my head around the logic of my seventeen-year-old daughter being the type of person described in the book. But, Allison sure liked the label. I don't know how many times since I have heard her referring to herself as a sex addict. Another way to gain people's attention?

Allison met with Mary several times a month for the next sixteen months. I can't say whether the talks with Mary slowed down Allison's behavior with boys or not, or if Allison just got better about hiding it all from me.

There was a third possibility, of course. Perhaps I just became desensitized to Allison's behavior. I think I learned to detach myself emotionally, over time, as a way to protect myself. Allison had worn me down, tired me out. Worrying wasn't going to make her change. I didn't want her to end up dead, like could have happened when she ran away from home to meet the predator in 2009, but I had to acknowledge the fact that Allison wasn't turning out to be the person I dreamed my daughter would be.

Giving up on her has never been an option, though.

Six

Prom

Before I found the mysterious envelope in the mailbox in February, and before the nightmare of house arrest began, Allison and Daniel had made plans to attend Allison's high school's prom together. I never went to my own high school prom, nor got married in a church with a pretty wedding dress, so Allison's prom morphed into something more important every day. It represented my success as a single parent, being able to purchase a pretty prom dress from the store for my daughter. It represented a chance for me to tangentially experience the magical night of dress-up little girls started looking forward to when they're young, a chance to reclaim some of Allison's innocence, youth, and normality of the American right-of-passage known as high school.

Thankfully, prom was in May. Allison and Daniel began making plans to attend prom in February, but were then forced into the no-contact zone of house arrest for forty-three days.

I have to admit I learned to respect Daniel quite a bit during those forty-three days of house arrest. Although he lived 200 miles away, and Allison could never *really* be sure how faithful he remained to the long-distance relationship he and Allison had together, he waited. I couldn't imagine any of the other boys Allison dated doing the same.

Finally, the day came when I could return Allison's cell phone. I smiled as I handed it over. I smiled as I watched her run down the stairs to her bedroom to call Daniel.

Allison was smiling when she finally re-surfaced from the basement. She also had a question. "Mom, Daniel wants to know if he can come prom dress shopping with us."

I had envisioned prom dress shopping as a special day between Allison and me, a real mother-daughter bonding event. Now Allison was asking if Daniel could horn in on my special day.

On the other hand, Daniel stuck with Allison during her forty-three days of house arrest. How many young men would willingly endure that for a seventeen-year-old girl? Joining us for a day of prom dress shopping could be my way of honoring his commitment to Allison. Besides, I still had wedding dress shopping with Allison to look forward to. Shopping for a prom dress together might be equally important to them.

During her forty-three-day ordeal of house arrest, Allison began receiving prom dress catalogs. Allison mooned over the pages of prom dresses in the catalogues. If this hadn't been my first-ever prom, I might have been smarter than to buy into the hype of having to drive to specialty bridal shops for a prom dress. I nearly kicked myself a year later when I saw comparable prom dresses at retailers like J.C. Penney and Herberger's. I nearly fell over when I saw the price difference. But, life is all about lessons learned.

MY MOTHER RAISED ME to be consciously aware of every penny spent. Over the years, I have tried to understand what her life was like growing up, but I still get angry when I realize my issues with money are a direct outcome of *her* issues with money.

Growing up, my mother taught me how to sew. People who don't sew tell me this is a wonderful skill to have mastered. What I can't explain is my love-hate relationship with sewing. My mother's objective for teaching my sister and me: we were *always* to sew our own clothes. The uniforms for school were purchased (I went to a kindergarten-through-eighth-grade parochial school—red polyester skirt, navy blue polyester vest, white cotton shirt), but everything else was homemade. I perfected my top-stitching so shirts were harder to recognize as homemade, but there was no such miracle for transforming the simple A-line cotton skirt.

Anything we would purchase, like winter jackets or blue jeans, were to be selected off the clearance racks in the basement of the department store where my mother had a credit card. No other options existed with my mother.

I'll never forget the light-brown suede-leather vest I bought with my retail store commission in high school, or the months it took me to buy a leather jacket with lay-a-way payments.

The only church wedding I ever participated in, I made a simple off-the-shoulder pink satiny dress. The bride and I met because we worked together in a fabric store. It was a small wedding. I was her only attendant.

I REMEMBER THE DAY Allison showed me the picture of her favorite prom dress from one of the catalogues. "Wow, that *is* a really pretty dress," I said. "How much is it, sweetie?"

"I don't know."

Of course she didn't know. Unlike the old Sears catalogue, these kept the price a secret. The purpose was to draw you into a specific store, for a specific dress. Like a bee to honey, or a moth to the light, it's too late when you hear the snap of the trap. "Isn't that dress lovely?" the store clerk will tell you with her sweetest smile. "It's only $750.00. But your daughter looks so elegant in it! She'll be the belle of the ball."

Instead of falling for the trap, I told Allison to call the store. "Just ask them how much prom dresses run, sweetie."

"I don't want to, Mom," she whined, almost like she already knew.

"Well, at least call and find out their store hours. If Daniel's going to join us, we want to make sure we plan to go when they're open."

The following weekend, Allison, Tommy, Daniel, and I walked into the first, and only, dress shop we needed for Allison's lovely—and expensive—prom dress.

We entered the wedding dress store, and immediately had to remove our shoes.

"Are you kidding?" I groaned quietly under my breath. I don't like walking around barefoot—or in this case, in stocking feet—in places that aren't my home. I'm not quite a germ-a-phobe, but I just have a thing about sharing other people's feet sweat.

It was also still snowy in our area, so I had worn my winter boots. I was worried about stepping into wet spots on the rug, which would result in wet socks for the rest of the day. I was worried about the odor that might linger in the air near my boots. I was worried about having chosen socks that morning with near-holes in the toes and heels.

A well-dressed sales clerk in her mid-twenties greeted us each with a smile, flipping her attention from me to Allison. "Can I help you?"

"Hi," Allison began with a grin spreading across her face from ear to ear. "I'm looking for this dress." Allison held up the page she ripped out of the catalogue, and showed it to the sales clerk.

"Uhm, let me check and see if we carry this one," the clerk began. "Can I take this for a minute?" she continued, taking the page Allison handed her.

As soon as the clerk turned away, Allison turned to me—with *the look*—the same look she'd been giving me since she was old enough to figure out how to bargain, the look that said, "Please, Mom, make it so."

I tried to prepare Allison for the worst. "Wow, there sure are lots of pretty dresses in here, Allison! Do you want to look around a little bit before you commit to one?"

"No, Mom, I want the one I showed you."

I turned away from Allison rather than getting drawn into the fight I knew was about to start. "Oh, wow, this one is really pretty!" I said in Allison's direction.

Allison cuddled up to Daniel while she waited for the clerk to come back.

When the clerk re-appeared, she wasn't alone. "Hi, I brought my manager over, so she can explain."

The manager gave us a quick lesson about the prom dress cataloguing industry. "They send out these catalogues to everyone, even though the individual stores decide which specific dresses to carry. We don't have that dress, but we do have lots of other designs and colors!"

Allison was crushed. She had dreamed of herself in that dress so long, she couldn't get the image of it out of her head—or keep the devastation from her face. The tears came quickly. She buried her face in Daniel's shoulder as the stream accelerated.

"I'm so sorry," the manager said before she artfully handed us back to the sales clerk. "If you have any questions about the dresses we *do* have here in the store, Cathy will be more than happy to answer them."

I thanked the manager for her help, then signaled the sales clerk my next move: I was going to look through the racks, giving Allison time to calm down with Daniel.

Five minutes later, Allison was willing to answer questions the sales clerk asked. "What about that particular dress did you like the most?" "What color were you thinking about for a dress?" "Would you like to try a couple on, just to see how they look?" "And what is the price range you're trying to stay within, Mom?"

Finally, Allison found the dress she liked the most. It was more expensive than I had hoped, but the $300.00 price was better than some of the others in the store.

"And this is for the prom here in town?" the sales clerk asked while Allison and I negotiated about the price tag.

"No, we're from . . ."

"I ask," the clerk continued, "because we make sure not to sell the same dress, in the same color, to anyone else from the same town as you. It would be horrible to end up at prom with someone else wearing the same dress, after you've spent so much money for it!"

I knew Allison well enough to know she would leave the prom, no matter what, if she saw another girl in the same dress. Rather than have something like that happen, I made the decision to buy the dress—and pay for it somehow.

Prom day. Daniel arrived shortly after noon, and I took some "Before" pictures of Allison and Daniel in their street clothes. I never had a big night like this; I wanted Allison to be able to look back fondly on every second of the day and night.

Allison and Daniel changed into their prom clothes about five, and sat on the couch next to each other, watching television, until it was time to go. I snapped some more photographs of them in the house, outside of the front door, and getting into Daniel's car, before heading off in my own car. Grand March was being held at the high school before the kids enjoyed their starlit night of dress-up and dancing at another location in town.

I sat alone in the high school auditorium. Tommy opted to stay at home rather than join me. I sat with my camera in my lap, waiting to hear Allison's and Daniel's names announced. I watched each couple promenade across the stage—thrilled knowing Allison was a part of it—and would have the memories forever.

Allison and Daniel were home before eleven, even though the prom was scheduled to last until midnight. Rather than question the early return, Tommy and I continued watching the movie we rented from the video store while Allison and Daniel headed downstairs to watch television before bedtime. (Daniel was to bunk with Tommy.)

I went to bed happy, knowing I had given Allison a night of beauty, fun, and being a teenager—just like everyone else at the prom.

SEVEN

A MOTHER'S DUTY

LIFE WASN'T SO BEAUTIFUL for me, though. I was storing a ton of secrets, and had to pass up a number of opportunities. Legally, I wondered, could I even talk to people about what was going on? If I could, which people would I even want to tell? Having no husband or boyfriend, my mother was next in line for close, familial support. But tell my mother *everything*? I was afraid revealing the truth about Allison would erode my self-esteem further. My mother raised her two daughters all alone, and we never got into trouble. I must be a failure, I rationalized, if my daughter was in serious legal trouble for the second time in her young life.

The option of telling my sister didn't feel much better. Living two states away, and busy with a career, I couldn't figure out a way to share my daily worries and frustrations over the telephone. Besides, in her role as the older sister, I was afraid she would take over again—like the time my car broke down on the way to a family funeral. Rather than drive the forty-five minutes to pick me and the kids up, my sister spent an hour locating a car-rental company, negotiating the rental (it was after-hours on a weekend) and a taxi service to shuttle me from my broken car to the car-rental office. The kids and I arrived at the funeral home for the wake five minutes before the end. The extra cost of the trip blew my budget for months.

My best option seemed to be my two best friends, Sara and Lindsey. Sara has three daughters, the oldest the same age as Allison. Sara and I met in a playgroup when the girls were about three years old. Although we don't see each other often anymore, we have been able to keep in touch pretty regularly, first through email, then through text messaging. Lindsey also has a daughter—gained through marriage. The value of Lindsey's input lies in the retrospective—Lindsey and her marriage have each survived, in spite of the many waves of traumatic behavior from her now married daughter. Lindsey lived further from me than Sara, though.

On the one hand, the distance from these women was nice. Text messaging people I rarely ever see brings a layer of honesty to the communication I might not have if they were sitting across the table. I wouldn't see the lowered eyelids as they listened to my latest challenge with Allison, I wouldn't see the disappointment for either me or Allison flash across their faces, I wouldn't hear heavy sighs slip out from their bodies as they prepared themselves to offer a response. On the other hand, their hands couldn't gently pat mine while I struggled to tell the story, their arms couldn't encircle me with an understanding hug, their eyes couldn't show how much of my pain they shared. All we had was the technological advance of text messaging, through which they both were accessible to me day and night—even if a reply came twenty-four hours later. Not advice, just a reply. Not advice, just encouragement that I'm a good mom. Not advice, just a virtual hug.

Not love that felt conditional, but love of friends who accept you just the way you are.

Loving support from my friends has helped me through some tough times, but it's never been a cure-all. Traveling helps, because it provides me a chance to escape the house and its slowly closing walls. It gives me a change of scenery. Traveling helps even more when I am aware of every tiny sound out in the street or in my driveway. Were the police going to come for Allison today? Was the doorbell going to ring, only to discover a predator at the door? To what lengths would I have to go to keep Allison safe?

Allison, Tommy, and I were planning on taking a trip with my mother during spring vacation of 2011, to visit a cousin and her family in another state, but Allison was under house arrest. I didn't know whether she could leave the state or not, and I was too afraid to ask.

While asking the public defender seemed like a logical course of action, the legacy of a controlling marriage dictated another course of action. Rather than have someone tell me, "No," and take away my freedom, I occasionally defer to a keeping-the-blinders-on course of action. If *I* made the decision to back out of the trip, I maintained the illusion of having some control over my life. If I asked the public defender and were told Allison could not leave the state for the trip, I would once again be the victim in my own life. Right or wrong, Tommy and my mother had to go without Allison and me. I have never asked my mother what explanation she gave the family, and she has never offered one. Again, I chose not to ask.

My cousin emailed pictures of the visit with Tommy. It's still hard to see those pictures of Tommy enjoying that spring vacation without Allison and me.

Attending the spring choir concert the following year was also difficult. As I watched Allison sing, I couldn't help but remember the concert the year before, the year Allison had been in police custody.

I STILL DEBATE about who I can or can't talk with about Allison's legal issues. On the one hand, I'm embarrassed to admit my child has done things society deems so awful and illegal, though television sit-coms and made-for-TV-movies explore the many layers of sex and technology daily.

On the other hand, predators live in the shadows of society. Predators groom their victims—young people just like Allison—promising them love in exchange for little intimacies like pictures.

I'm ultimately afraid people will continue blaming me for Allison's actions, without getting the full story. Single mothers have been portrayed as loose women by too many television shows and movies over the years, though I haven't had a single date (or relations with anyone) since my divorce. When I turn on the television, or encounter some religious people in the context of my life, I'm left with the impression they still advocate a woman's place as being in the home, raising the family, while the husband provides for his family's needs. Would they think I'm bad, then, because I initiated the divorce that ended my marriage of twelve years? Would they call me an unfit mother because I'd gone out into the world to pursue a career, rather than focusing on finding a replacement husband?

Would they judge me, based solely on the actions of my daughter, or would they honor me for my hard work and tireless efforts to hold everything together?

"Has Allison ever been molested?" the police investigator asked me in March of 2011.

"That's what she says," I replied almost immediately.

By June of 2013, I realized Allison had accused nearly everyone but me, Tommy, my mother, and my sister of sexually molesting her. I'd only been accused of physically abusing her.

I guess my single-ness has been a God-send. What if I *had* gotten involved with a man, I began to wonder. Would Allison have accused him of sexually abusing her when she eventually got mad at him about something?

I could have ruined an innocent man's life, all in the name of loving my daughter.

I would have ruined an innocent man's life, all because I would be honoring the code of believing whatever my daughter tells me.

Has Allison ever been molested?

Part Two

Senior Year

EIGHT

TO WHAT LENGTHS . . .

TWO DAYS BEFORE SHE finished her junior year of high school, Allison sent me a text message saying she wanted to move again. Allison told me she was fed up with the name-calling and harassment she encountered every day at the high school, and the only solution she could think of was to start all over again somewhere new. She wouldn't take responsibility for creating those problems, though.

It's hard to say if I would have moved again; teaching doesn't allow for quick changes the way other careers might. For college teachers, the hiring season for full-time, tenure-track positions typically begins in October, and ends in March or April of the following year when offers are made and accepted. Because Allison didn't introduce the topic until the beginning of June, the only teaching jobs I might have been able to get would have been of a temporary, non-benefit-earning semester-long variety.

Not to mention the logistics of selling our current house, so I could buy—or rent—another place to live in the new town.

Additionally, there was the tiny matter of the promise I had made Allison and Tommy when we moved to this town from Wyoming. "I promise I won't move you again until you are *both* out of high school." Tommy was just starting to get comfortable in the high school, as he thought about being a sophomore rather than a freshman. He was just starting to get involved with extra-curricular activities he liked and needed to be comfortable knowing he wouldn't be starting all over again somewhere else. Allison needed to understand how committed I am when I make a promise.

Instead of moving, I talked to the psychiatrist Allison had been seeing off-and-on (she was diagnosed with ADHD-Combined Type as a child). I asked him to set the ADHD diagnosis aside and run Allison through a new battery of diagnostic tests. After testing in the ninetieth percentile for depression, Allison began a double-pronged regimen of anti-depressant medication and talk-therapy. I spent the summer fighting with Allison about returning to the high school for her senior year rather than going to live with her boyfriend and his family in another town (to be "taken care of" by another family and attend a different high school). I spent the summer driving her from doctor appointment to doctor appointment. I spent the summer trying to enjoy the individuals my seventeen-year-old daughter and fifteen-year-old son had become. I spent the summer bracing myself for the last moments I had to educate and empower my teenage daughter who already had one foot out the door.

Allison wasn't happy about it, but in August she finally accepted the fact she would be heading back to one last year of high school in our town while living in my house. At seventeen, she was frustrated by the amount of control she felt I had over her life—but wouldn't get a job, a normal step towards independence.

In the middle of her senior year, Allison celebrated her eighteenth birthday. Being deemed a legal adult changed everything for—and with—Allison. I was unprepared for how hard she was going to push the boundaries. I was shocked and saddened to discover what Allison's priorities were.

I also learned most of Allison's communications were by text message, rather than actual, face-to-face conversations.

Nine

September—Suspended?

I remember Allison's very first day of school. She was dressed in a pretty pink jumper, a white short-sleeved shirt underneath, white bobby socks, black patent-leather Mary Jane shoes, pigtails—and a nearly empty pink backpack on her shoulders.

I didn't cry on Allison's first day of school—and she didn't either. Both of us were too excited for the adventure of school to begin. Both of us were ready for her to spread her wings, make new friends, and learn about the world.

I nearly cried the first day of her senior year, though. My little girl had grown up into a beautiful young woman, had survived in spite of the odds she seemed to like playing against, and was going to be flying from the nest when the school year ended.

Allison sent me a text message at 1:40 p.m. on September 12, 2011: "I got suspended for the rest of the day. I'm going to have someone take me home."

At 1:51 p.m., another text message: "I can't leave without them knowing you said yes."

When I finally viewed these two messages at two, and called Allison back, she had already left the high school. "Bobby is giving me a ride home," she reported.

"Okay," I replied. "I will open the garage door for you."

"Oh, you're home?" Allison asked with surprise. "Can I hang out with Bobby for a while? I just need to calm down," she continued.

"Just come home," I said with as much patience as I could muster. "I have to go back to work in a few minutes."

"Well, Bobby just told me he has horses. I want to go see them. Just leave the back door unlocked. I'll come home after I see his horses."

I didn't like this arrangement, but needed to remain calm. I had to go back to work and teach one more class for the day. I had also been working on keeping my blood pressure down. I was trying to keep myself from getting sucked into the drama Allison daily creates.

I headed to the garage, and called the high school principal.

"Hi, it's Jeanette Lukowski. Can I—"

"Hello! How are you," the principal cheerily asked.

"Oh, I'm . . ." what? What was I? Frazzled? Frustrated? Fed up? "Allison just called and said she was suspended because of a backpack violation. Can we meet tomorrow morning, the three of us, to figure this out?"

"What do you mean she's suspended?" he asked. "Did Ms. Winters explain why?"

"No, Allison's the one who called and told me."

"Oh, that's not our policy at all," Mr. Stewart said. "Let me check with Ms. Winters about what happened, and give you a call back. Is this a good number for you?"

Six minutes later, my phone rang. "Hi, Jeanette, this is Ms. Winters. Allison isn't suspended. We, in fact, had a really nice talk. She came in crying, was able to calm down, and left the office."

No one was aware Allison had already left the building.

The first day of the second week of school, and I was already stressing out about Allison's behavior. How in the world was I going to get through the rest of the school year if this was how it started?

Of equal importance, though, how did Allison leave the building without anyone knowing?

WHEN I WAS in high school, we had what was called a closed campus. There were two main entrance doors to the school, one at the front, and the other on nearly the opposite end of the school. Both were unlocked in the morning so students could enter. Once the school day began, though, the only door to remain unlocked from the outside was the door near the main office. If students were to enter after school started, they had to stop in the office for an admission slip. If students were to leave the school before the end of the day, they had to stop in the office to sign out. There was one hundred percent accountability for every student, every day, as far as I ever knew. No one could sneak out of the numerous other exit doors without sounding an alarm. They were emergency-exit doors, and they were well monitored.

Is the difference between *my* high school's level of security and accountability and Allison's high school's apparent *lack* of security and accountability simply the difference between a high school in Chicago and one in the north woods of Minnesota?

Angry because Allison was able to leave the high school building so easily, and without anyone's knowledge, I also knew I couldn't blame the school administrators or staff. Allison was the one I needed to hold accountable.

TEN

OCTOBER— A NEW BEST FRIEND

I WALKED DOWNSTAIRS at 7:00 a.m. to wake Allison up for school the morning of October 26th.

"I have such a huge migraine," she whispered from her bed. "I was up all night, and only got two hours of sleep."

"Why were you up all night?" I asked, remaining as calm as I could.

"Daniel called. He wanted to talk, and then I cried for a while."

Daniel and Allison had been dating for over a year. Allison claimed to have initiated a break-up the week before, but Daniel wouldn't accept it.

I walked back upstairs, simmering with anger because Allison wouldn't get out of bed. I had to drive Tommy to school, though, because he had an extra curricular activity for an hour before school.

While Tommy got out of the car at school at 7:25 a.m., I sent a text message to Allison. "I think it's important for you to go to school the last day of the week." Even though it was only Wednesday, the kids were going to be home from school Thursday and Friday, due to some district-wide activity slated for the teachers.

Allison's reply came two minutes later. "So I have to go to school?"

I wanted to throttle her through the phone. Instead, I drove home, and continued getting ready for work. While I didn't bother going downstairs to try and motivate Allison out of bed anymore, I also didn't tiptoe through the house.

At 8:15 a.m., I left the still-quiet house for work.

Allison sent me a text message at 10:26 a.m., but I wouldn't see it until I finished my 11:00 a.m. class. "When is your class over?"

"Which?" I send back to Allison as I walked to the car in the parking lot. In addition to my full-time teaching job, I had another part-time teaching job across town. That class began at 12:30 p.m.

"I don't know," her reply began. "I thought I was going to go to school."

"I thought you were too."

"I don't know how to get there?"

Allison began driving with a permit soon after she passed the written test when she was fifteen. I felt it was my duty to provide the children with the money for the classroom instruction portion of driving school, but didn't want to pay for the mandatory behind-the-wheel instruction needed for anyone seeking their license between sixteen and eighteen. Since we only had the one car—a used 1993 Mitsubishi Expo—Allison could drive *with* me whenever she asked, but she would never be taking it out alone. Getting their own car, separate auto insurance, and driver's license before they turned eighteen would be each child's individual responsibility. One of the many difficult decisions every parent—especially a single parent living without child support—must make for him/herself. Allison wouldn't get a job, though. Instead, Allison relied on me, and a wide variety of high school friends, to give her rides to and from school.

Just before I left the parking lot, I sent Allison a reply. "Call one of the many people who give you rides home, I guess."

"No one can come over now, because they are all in class."

"I am too," I replied angrily. "On Mondays, Wednesdays, and Fridays, this semester."

Feeling vindicated, as a mother, I resumed the conversation with Allison at 1:25 p.m., when my 12:30 p.m. class was over. "So now I'm free 'til 2:25 p.m."

I was surprised by Allison's response a minute later. "I'd still go to school."

Really? Why? The school day is nearly over.

Or, was Allison only bluffing? Rather than try to figure it out, I sent a reply right away. "Ready then?"

Three minutes later, Allison replied with a simple "Yes."

"Okay," I sent back before starting the car. "Grab me an apple, please, and I'll be there in ten minutes."

I dropped Allison off at the high school at about 2:00 p.m., and headed back across town to teach one more class at 2:30 p.m.

When I was done with the last class at 3:25 p.m., I sent Allison a text to let her know I was heading back over to the high school to pick her up.

"I'm at the store with Katie."

For the second time in one day, I wanted to throttle Allison. How could she think it was okay to take off with Katie after school, when she had only been to school for the last hour? According to my parenting rules, Allison's claim of a headache bad enough to make her miss school was the equivalent of staying home sick. If a child stayed home from school for a sick day, the child didn't get to leave the house the rest of the day. So where, exactly, did a trip to the mall with her girlfriend fit into the equation? Rather than explode at Allison through the phone, I sent her a very simple text message at 3:30 p.m.: "Oh!"

"I talked to Mrs. Klein," Allison sent at 3:35 p.m.

I guess I was supposed to forgive the trip to the mall because Allison talked to one of her many teachers in the hour she attended school.

On Halloween, the kids returned to school after their five-day weekend. I got done with class at 3:25 p.m., and sent Allison the daily text message about being on my way to pick her up from the high school.

When I got to the high school fifteen minutes later, and didn't see Allison, I called her phone.

"Oh," Allison answered, focusing her reply to the message of my text. "Katie and I are going to get some food, and then hang out at the mall. I should be home at like 6:00 p.m."

I was hearing about Katie for the second time in five days. I realized Katie must have a car. Katie must be Allison's new best friend.

By 6:35 p.m., when Allison still wasn't home from school, I called her again. "Oh, we're over at the college, passing out Halloween candy. I'll be home around nine," Allison coolly purred into the phone.

I didn't like the inconsiderate way Allison was treating me. I didn't like the fact she was once again missing dinner. Tommy, Allison, and I might be a small family, but having dinner together as a family had *always* been important to me.

I was also annoyed because Allison had said she didn't want to go to college next year—yet she was spending so much time over there hanging out, using the Internet in the campus library, and now passing out candy to trick-or-treaters. Instead of going to college next year, Allison was planning to move back to the town in Wyoming she (and Tommy) talked me into moving away from between her eighth and ninth grades. She planned on living with Carl, the first boy she kissed at twelve. Carl was the first boy she tells people she had sex with at thirteen, the young man of nineteen who had a child by another young woman a year or two earlier. According to Allison, Carl was going to let her live in his home and give her a car to drive around, in exchange for cooking and cleaning.

MY MOTHER PUSHED ME to go to college. I turned eighteen a few weeks before I was dropped off at a small Lutheran college in southern Minnesota. It was a long drive, but I agreed to it because I didn't see any difference between an empty apartment in Chicago and a college dorm in Minnesota.

The only time my dad ever said he was proud of me, it was written in a letter my mother sent to me at that college. One line, added to the end of a letter my mother had written to me, and then carried with her to the nursing home. One line, received too late in my life.

Before cell phones, I couldn't afford long distance phone calls to friends for support, so I withered.

Without a constant flow of return letters from Hans, addressing any of the topics I had written to him about, I shriveled.

Without any place in town to walk to after six o'clock at night, I died.

I spent one semester at the school in southern Minnesota before I returned home. My mom had me attending a community college downtown days later.

A similar pattern occurred the next year, but this time it was my sister's *Alma Mater* in southern South Dakota. A bigger school, I had hope—until my roommate hated me. Was it because I had a job at the campus library, mandating I be an early-riser compared to her night-owl nature? Or was it because I wasn't the same type of person she had heard my sister was?

Once again, I was headed back to the downtown college in Chicago after a January return home.

I finally got my mom to hear me say I didn't want her running my life when I got married to Frank. We eloped to city hall two days after my twenty-first birthday—and spent the first several years of our marriage tied to a military base in northwestern West Germany.

I didn't return to college until after we moved to Minnesota in 1991. I paid a bit more money for tuition, but I was fully committed to the effort a college education demands. And I went on to earn three different degrees by 2011.

I WANTED ALLISON to go to college, but I knew better than to push her. But, to go back to Wyoming to live with Carl?

ELEVEN

NOVEMBER—WEDDING TALK

I WAS EXCITED WHEN Allison sent me a mid-day text message from school that said: "December 6 is cap and gown ordering day."

Hours later, I was cringing.

Allison and I were home together watching something on television when a commercial came on for a new collection of wedding rings at a jewelry store.

"Oh, I love that ring!" Allison gushed.

I wanted to tell her there would be plenty of other rings on television commercials before she needed to be picking one out, but wisely kept the thought to myself.

Shortly after eight-thirty, out of left field, Allison said, "So I told Carl about the wedding ring I saw. I told him that's the one I want."

Again, I held my tongue. How could she be thinking—and talking—about wedding rings with a boy she hadn't seen in over three years?

Fifteen minutes later, we were in the bathroom, next to each other by the sink. "I don't know what I'm going to do without you, Mom. I'll be calling you all of the time, asking about this or that."

Taking her conversational lead, I tried asking a question that had been on my mind since Allison began texting and talking to Carl again in September. "Will Carl talk to me, or at least look at me, when I take you out there?"

Allison laughed. "Of course, Mom. You're invited to the wedding."

Wedding. Why did each conversation keep circling back to either babies or weddings, rather than formal (December 2nd), prom (May), graduation, and career plans?

I couldn't think about marriage and babies.

Tommy walked into the bathroom as I brushed my teeth before bed. "Allison is planning on getting married," he said.

"Really," was all I could manage to say.

"Yeah, we were talking about it," he continued. "She said, 'If all goes well on December 12th, Carl and I are going to get married.' I asked her what December 12th was about, and she said, 'Carl goes back to court.' I asked her for what, and she said, 'Rape.'"

My head started to spin. Carl was facing charges for rape? And Allison knew about it?

Was Carl innocent of his crime like Allison had been of hers?

FRANK WAS NEVER ROMANTIC. I was able to see the signs in hindsight, but I wasn't able to when I met him at nineteen, or married him two days after my twenty-first birthday. I just focused on the details like how his mother had died when he was fourteen, and his father was blind.

Frank never really proposed to me, so much as he made the proposal a game of liar's poker. "What would you say if I asked you to marry me?" he said one night while I was trying to close out the cash register of the fabric store. I was one of the two assistant managers. I was the person in charge that night.

"Ask me when you're serious," I said, without looking up from the cash drawer.

"I am serious. What would you say?"

The game went a couple more rounds like that, making me lose count of the cash each time, and forcing me to start over again.

"What would you say?"

"Fine," I finally answered. "Now, can I focus so we can get out of here?"

Frank never presented me with an engagement ring. I had to buy the wedding rings myself, with my own Sears credit card. I settled on a pretty ring set for myself—separate engagement ring with the tiniest diamond, and a wedding band the same width and design as the engagement ring—and a band of a different style and color for Frank. (I prefer yellow-gold, he wanted white-gold.)

Frank could never commit to a date, and neither of us had money for a wedding. We eloped, to City Hall, two days after my best friend got married.

Frank was three hours late picking me up that morning.

THE KIDS AND I DROVE to the Metrodome in Minneapolis—home of the Minnesota Vikings—to watch our high school football team play in the state play-offs on November 18th. The team had been undefeated during regular season play, a first since the 1950s, I was told. Tommy, an avid fan all season, told me "they've made it to the quarter-finals like the last five years, but they've never made it past."

Although there were fan-bus opportunities for people who wanted to go to the game, the twenty-five dollars per person was too much for my household budget. Besides, this seemed like a great opportunity for some family bonding time: 1) The run-for-state would forever be a part of Allison's senior year, and she knew boys who were on the football team, 2) Tommy was friends with a few of the boys on the team, and 3) one of the football players was enrolled in my college literature course (post-secondary enrollment option). I took the day off work, and the three of us drive down for the Friday, 12:45 p.m. game.

After the game, Allison asked to be dropped off at the apartment where one of the boys she attended middle school with was living. Although she hadn't seen him in six years, they'd reconnected via an Internet social networking site a few months earlier. I agreed to the stop, thinking it would be a visit of an hour or two like she'd had with her other friends. I dropped her off at 4:45 p.m., and Tommy and I drove over to the mall. An hour later, Allison sent me a text message. "I'll get a ride."

I was surprised by the message. "Get a ride where?" I sent back.

"To Grandma's" Allison replied.

On the surface, this seemed like a really nice offer. Even though Tommy and I had just stopped to buy concession-stand pretzels in the mall, we were both still very hungry—and bored in the mall, as we had no money to buy anything other than food. But Grandma's house was an hour's drive northwest. I wanted to ask Allison why this boy, who she hadn't seen in six years, was willing to drive two hours, round trip, just for the opportunity to visit a bit longer, after Daniel, the boy she had been dating for seventeen months, hadn't always been willing to do the same thing. I wanted to ask, but I also wanted to be released from the boredom of the mall. I wanted to trust my daughter. I wanted to let her feel more like the adult she was thirty-five days away from being.

I sent back a text message saying "Okay," and Tommy and I left the mall.

By 10:34 p.m., I was exhausted. I wanted to go to sleep, but couldn't relinquish the role of parent-waiting-up-for-teenage-child to my mother. So, I sent Allison a text. "Coming yet?"

Two minutes later, I received Allison's reply. "Not yet."

I was angry. Allison had set me up. She was sitting an hour's drive away, and she knew I was too tired to want to drive back and get her.

I dozed off, then, in an upright position, sitting on the couch. An hour later, I was awakened by a text message from Allison. "I have the flu coming out both ends."

I recognized it as an excuse, but still expected Allison to return that evening. I took my contact lenses out, but wouldn't change into pajamas or open up the sofa sleeper because it would block access to the front door. Instead, I grabbed my pillow, turned off the television, and spread an afghan over my outstretched legs on the couch.

The next time I woke up, the house was dark and quiet. I reached for my cell phone, rather than getting up from the couch, and discovered it was 3:30 a.m. No word from Allison since her flu excuse at 11:30 p.m. I got up, walked into the bathroom, and fired off an angry text message to Allison: "Real nice of you—thanks."

She didn't respond.

Since changing into pajamas after sleeping through half of the night in my clothes seemed silly, and opening up the sofa sleeper would make too much noise (Tommy was in his sleeping bag on the living room floor), I resumed my place on the couch with the afghan.

At 7:19 a.m. the next morning, I sent Allison one last angry text: "By the way, my vehicle heads north after my haircut—hope you make it here before then."

Allison's reply didn't come until 9:03 a.m. "When's your haircut?"

I never received an apology, just another excuse. "Everyone fell asleep around 1:00 a.m."

At some point during our quiet three-hour drive home, Allison said, "He started drinking right after I got there, which is why I couldn't get a ride last night."

"I'm glad you didn't take the risk of drinking and driving," I began, "but then why did you say you would get a ride to Grandma's? Your brother and I were waiting, purposely, just fifteen minutes away. I was going to come back and pick you up, dear."

Perhaps there is still hope for you, Allison, if I can just figure out the right things to say to get through to you.

I DIDN'T LIKE the idea of Allison connecting with a boy from middle school if she had plans to move to Wyoming in six or seven months, but I didn't like the idea of her moving back to Wyoming either.

As much as I hated to acknowledge them, I was starting to see similarities between Allison and her father. Allison wasn't taking responsibility for her actions (lying) any more than Frank. Frank was supposedly engaged to a girl when I met him—and never broke it off with her until we were married.

I remember Frank's dad telling him the girl had stopped by the house a week or two after we eloped. Frank called her, made plans to meet with her somewhere nearby and didn't want me going with him.

FOUR DAYS LATER, I received what I hoped was a ray of sunshine in the thunderous life Allison had been presenting me. We were driving to school together, alone—I had dropped Tommy off an hour earlier for a before-school activity.

"I'm really excited about the future, but kind of scared, too," Allison said out of the blue.

"Everybody feels that way, dear. We're excited by the possibilities, but fear the unknown. It's okay to feel that way. There are so many possibilities in front of you when you graduate high school."

Or is it already too late?

THANKSGIVING. The kids and I were home, alone. We slept in, I cooked everyone's favorite foods, we ate, and were enjoying a quiet afternoon of television movies together when I happened to glance over at Allison's cell phone while she was texting someone. I saw the name "Mark," and an area code I didn't recognize. The message seemed innocent enough, a simple "Happy Thanksgiving" greeting, but who was Mark, and where was that area code from?

Several hours later, I got the answer. Mark's number was an Akron, Ohio, area code.

Allison was twenty-nine days away from her eighteenth birthday. There wasn't much I could say, or do about Mark from Ohio.

I had no concrete evidence, either. Mark was just a name I had seen on Allison's cell phone while sitting next to her on the couch Thanksgiving afternoon.

I WAS SEVENTEEN before I had my first serious boyfriend. We met on my seventeenth birthday, as a matter of fact. His name was Ben.

Ben was two years older than I was and had his own car. He lived with his family in a house about five miles from the apartment building my family lived in. He had graduated high school the year before and was doing small contract jobs with a construction company when we met.

Ben and I dated, exclusively, for a year and a half. We broke up after I went to college in Minnesota. I actually broke up with Ben, because I didn't see us wanting the same kind of future. He wanted a stay-at-home wife, who would cook, clean, and take care of the kids like his mother did. I wanted a career.

Frank was my next boyfriend.

THE HIGH SCHOOL football team won their semi-final game in the state play-offs. We returned to the Metrodome for the championship game on Saturday, November 26th. Tommy's friend joined us for the trip, and got permission to spend the night with us at my mother's house since the game started at 3:00 p.m.

Allison and I chatted during the drive down, sat together at the game, and made jokes all the way back to the parking lot. Never a hint of the plans Allison made with the boy again, until I was driving the downtown streets back to the highway.

"You're not pulling the same number you did last week," I quickly told her. "We have Tommy's friend."

We dropped Allison off at 6:45 p.m., and I told her we would be back for her at 9:00—which would get us back to my mother's house by ten. Then Tommy, his friend, and I head to a favorite fast-food place near the mall to eat, followed by a short drive to the mall to kill some time.

Once again, the mall was boring. In spite of its being Black Friday, none of us had money, so we headed back to the apartment for Allison. At 8:45 p.m., I sent Allison a text from the apartment parking lot.

"Thirty more minutes, please," Allison sent back.

"I'm not going to just sit here and waste gas, dear," I replied. If it were warm enough outside to unroll the windows, perhaps I could have waited patiently. But I also didn't feel like having Allison dictate the schedule for the family.

"Go to the mall," Allison suggested.

"That's where we just came from," I sent back.

"The grocery store?" Allison continued. "I'm hungry."

And I'm tired of this, Allison. I don't want to play this game.

A cloyingly-sweet odor followed Allison into the car. "What is that smell?" I asked her.

"Smoke," Allison quickly replied. "Everyone was smoking."

"Uhm, that's not smoke, dear," I said as I pulled out of the parking lot. My dad smoked unfiltered Camel cigarettes my whole life. I used to sneak cigarettes from his packs when I started. Frank smoked menthols when I met him, but switched over to my brand when we began dating. I smoked cigarettes for about ten years; I know the smell of cigarette smoke.

The smell also didn't dissipate an iota during the hour-long drive back to my mother's house. In fact, it got so nauseating by the end, I was afraid I would have to open the car windows in spite of the twenty-degree temperature outside.

Allison wouldn't acknowledge her inebriated behavior that night. She didn't complain about the television set two feet from her head while we watched *Saturday Night Live*. She didn't explain why she got up at 1:30 the next morning to make herself a glass of chocolate milk—the same hangover remedy my mother told me Allison drank the morning she came home with the "flu" weeks earlier.

I never took Allison to see that boy again. While I know a large number of teens drink before reaching their twenty-first birthday, I was especially angry with Allison because of her total disregard of me, my values, and how it would reflect back on me if/when Tommy's sixteen-year-old friend were to talk about the trip at home.

I HAD MY BOUT with alcohol when I was Allison's age, but I was basically living alone at the time. After the incident with my dad and the hammer, he was moved to a nursing home. My sister was away at college in South Dakota, my mom had three jobs and would visit Dad in the nursing home every weekend. If she worked too late in the day on Saturday, or was too tired to visit him after work, she would drive to the nursing home on Sunday after church.

I drank socially, but I drank because I was home, alone, probably ninety percent of the time.

I don't think my mom ever noticed my drinking. Was it because I never went home drunk, like Allison? Or was it because my mom was too tired to notice me after a week of working and taking care of my dad?

I stopped the heavy drinking six months after I started. I still can't remember the night Ben said he picked me up from a party, drove me to his friend's house to hang out, and stopped on the way back to my house so I could throw up at the curb (even pointing out the spot the next day—complete with the napkins he'd given me to wipe my face).

NOVEMBER 30TH. Allison and I were on our way home from school when she announced, "Katie and I are planning on taking a road trip sometime in spring, but before graduation. We're obviously going to wait until January . . ." the unstated implication being "after I turn eighteen." "Then, of course, we need to wait until after the snow . . . but sometime before May."

You mean sometime between when you no longer need my *permission, but before you move to Wyoming, get married, and need your husband's permission?*

Having released the smarmy thought, I tried for a calmer approach two blocks later. "I really wish you wouldn't focus so heavily on this marriage plan. You were dating Daniel for over a year, and you couldn't predict how ugly he would get over your break-up. How do you think you know Carl well enough to go out there and marry him when you haven't even seen each other in over three years?"

Allison muttered, "I don't even know what I'm doing anymore."

I let it go, and drove the rest of the way home in silence. Perhaps the plan with Carl was fading all on its own? I chided myself to be more patient—and quiet. Perhaps I could still gently guide Allison in the right direction, as long as I didn't push.

TWELVE

DECEMBER—WEDDING PLANS

On December 5th, Allison climbed into the car after school, shut the car door, and said, "Susie and I would like to go to Grand Rapids sometime this week. When would be a good day?"

"I don't know, dear," was all I could muster. I wanted to support her interest in a new friendship, especially with a girl, but couldn't imagine what interest the town an hour away would hold for the girls. Instead, I focused on pulling away from the curb and exiting the chaos known as the high school's parking lot at the end of the day.

"It's just that Susie and I want to go to the dress shop. They have such pretty dresses there," Allison continued in her cheery chirp.

"They're not going to just let you girls try dresses on, you know. It's not like when you and your friends go to the mall, dear."

"Mom," Allison began, then paused. "Carl and I are getting married."

Just like that.

"He told me to pick a date," Allison continued, plunging into the silence enveloping our car's interior.

I drove home, on auto-pilot, and focused my energy on staying calm.

Although I wanted to take Allison by the shoulders, and shake some sense into her when we got home, the constant fear she would simply walk out the door on her eighteenth birthday kept my arms tethered to my sides. I wasn't going to give her an excuse to leave. Instead, I took off my shoes, hung my coat in the hall closet, and made myself a salad before sitting down at the dining room table to face Allison.

"Carl said I could have a small ring and a big wedding, or an expensive ring and a small wedding. I'm going with the big ring and a small wedding because then I can have the ring all the time. He's letting me make all of the decisions for our wedding. He doesn't care about any of it. He just wants me to be happy," Allison gushed, almost all in one breath.

I listened to everything Allison said, looking up from my salad bowl every so often, and nodding my head if I agreed with something in particular.

"I just don't know what all I need to do, Mom, and would really like your help."

"Okay," I said, getting up from the table. *I can play this game. Perhaps flooding you with information will make you throw your hands up and walk away like you did when you were a child.* "I want you to find some paper, and make notes. There are a lot of options with a wedding. It all depends on what you want to spend your money on. First, though, you have to talk with the pastor of whatever church you want to get married in. If you are getting married here, you'd talk to our pastor. If you are getting married there, you'll have to talk to the pastor that took over at the church we were going to when we lived there."

Carl was living in Wyoming; we lived in Minnesota. We moved to Wyoming in 2006. Allison met Carl within our first week. Then we moved back to Minnesota in 2008. Although she told me they talk "all of the time" on the telephone, or via an Internet social networking site, Allison and Carl hadn't spent any time together in the past three-and-a-half years.

"Once you've spoken with the pastor, then you need to decide if you want a reception or not, and where you would like that to take place. Some churches will let you rent out their space, like a Fellowship Hall, and maybe even hire some of the ladies from the congregation to cook and serve your meal, or you can rent out a facility. Like Jim and Sally's wedding this summer—they rented tents for the back yard, had the ladies from Sally's church come out and cook for them, and bought paper plates and plastic forks for eating. Mark and Laura, on the other hand, went to a church they don't belong to, rented that room at the resort, and Laura's mom made all of the table decorations.

"That's often the hardest part. Getting the wedding and reception place and date settled. Now, will you want a reception, with dancing? Then you need a DJ. Do you want to have an open bar, a cash bar, or no alcohol at all? Pete and Cindy had drink coupons at their wedding last year, remember? But they also went around and poured everyone one glass of wine for the toasting part. Oh, but you and Carl aren't even old enough yet, so maybe you don't want a bar part at all."

"An open bar doesn't seem like a good idea," Allison said. "That just creates more drunk people, since they'll drink more."

"You're right about that one, dear. It's also a very expensive option.

"So, church, reception, what else? Photographers tend to have package prices, kind of like for senior pictures. Decorations for the tables. Flowers—you'll have two sets of flowers. There's the bouquet that you carry with you, and then the bouquet you throw away."

"Yeah," Allison said. "I was thinking about daisies or something for the tables. Something kind of cheap."

"And then you have to have take-home things for all of the guests, at the table. Jim and Sally didn't have anything, but Mark and Laura had those cute little things her mom made, remember? You'll also need gifts for your bridal party. The girls get some kind of jewelry, like a pretty necklace they all wear, so that everybody matches. The guys get something else. I don't know. Maybe something like a fancy money clip or something you could engrave? Something.

"So church, reception, flowers, music, food—oh, cake! You can have one cake, or several smaller cakes like Jim and Sally had, or choices like Mark and Laura had, or cupcakes like Jeff and Karen had. Do you remember their wedding?" I think Allison had been eleven.

All the time I rattled off wedding-planning details, Allison took notes. Part of me was waiting for her to throw her hands up in the air, like the child I still remember her being, and announce "This is too much. I quit. Packing for college will be easier than this," but she didn't. Allison had instead fallen into student mode, furiously taking notes while her teacher lectured about the upcoming test. The other part of me wanted to make Allison see how expensive a wedding would be, so my argument about needing a college education in order to make a livable wage in 2011 would make more sense to the child whose only experience with "work" was the once-a-month night of babysitting for the family two houses down.

"Wow, that's a lot of stuff," Allison finally said after my extended silence. "I'm going to have to email all of this to Carl, and tell him I need his help with some of this."

Test number one of the pending marriage?

The following morning, Allison placed her graduation cap, gown, and tassel order at school.

"With shipping and handling and tax," her text message read, "the total on cap and gown order is $71.71."

Coming on the heels of the conversation we had about weddings the night before, I wished I could get Allison to see the realities of financial adulthood. A required graduation cap, gown, and plain tassel, items probably never worn more than once, cost $24.95. The additional package of twenty-five fancy graduation announcements she wanted, and a mini-tassel key chain for the lone house key she carried—including tax, shipping, and handling—cost just over seventy dollars. Did she understand how much a wedding would cost?

Driving home from school in the afternoon, I had another encounter with the bubbly version of Allison. "So, I was doing a lot of research on the Internet this morning, and I've got a lot of information for the wedding. I also sent an email to the new pastor of the church we went to. It took me a while to figure out which one it was."

As we sat at home, eating our afternoon snacks, Allison continued. "I was thinking we would have sloppy joes for the wedding dinner. Sloppy joes, and veggies with dip and stuff. Does that sound like a good idea? Sloppy joes are even cheaper than chicken, after all."

It sounded more like a child's birthday party menu than a wedding reception meal, but I kept my mouth shut.

Allison's plan was to get married in July. I wanted to ask her why she felt the need to rush it, but reminded myself the brain of a seventeen-year-old wasn't fully developed yet. At seventeen, mid-life might be twenty-five, with "old" being located somewhere in one's thirties.

"So, when can we go look at wedding dresses?"

I reminded Allison I had no money for anything wedding related. I explained my ability to pay for high school graduation expenses, perhaps college applications . . .

"That's okay, Mom. I already told you, Carl's paying for it."

"How is that going to work, dear? He's there, and you're here."

"Well, can't we go and try some dresses on?"

Rather than continue down the track heading us into another fight, I handed Allison the business card I picked up from the shop when we bought her prom dress last spring.

"Thanks, Mom," Allison chirped while extracting her cell phone from her back pocket.

"They said we have to make an appointment, Mom."

"Just get the information you want for right now." *In other words, find out what kind of down payment and date commitment the store will want before they just let you try on dresses, dear.*

"I'll have to call you back," Allison said into her phone.

The next day, Allison sent me another mid-day text message from school: "Got an appointment scheduled for wedding dresses January 14, at noon."

I had nothing to say.

Just after five that evening, Allison's cell phone vibrated with an incoming call. Uncharacteristically, she stayed on the couch next to me and answered the phone. "It's Dad!" she quietly mouthed to me. They hadn't spoken in several months.

The conversation began with a discussion of plans for Allison's birthday. She wanted to get a tattoo for her eighteenth birthday, but

I wouldn't take her, or pay for it. I don't like tattoos. I grew up looking at too many ugly blue ones staining my father's body.

After she hung up, Allison confessed to telling Frank she had some news. "No, Dad, I'm not pregnant," she shared with me, then explained she didn't tell him over the phone. "I emailed it to him. He can read it in the email."

Did Allison want someone to tell her not to marry Carl?

More specifically, did Allison want her *dad* to tell her not to marry Carl?

I began to wonder how truly manipulative my daughter was. The question of *Nature vs. Nurture* again.

I FIRST HEARD about *Nature vs. Nurture* in college. I think I was enrolled in a psychology class at the time.

My cousin had twin girls the same year I gave birth to Tommy, so the *Nature vs. Nurture* question took on a new edge for me. Having never grown up with brothers, I would now be able to examine birth-order, gender, and twins all at the same time, thanks to the close age of Allison, Tommy, and the identical twins.

I chose to support the *Nurture* camp all the years I single-parented the children. Fifteen years later, I started to accept *Nature*—one's genetic coding—holds more cards in who a person will be than how well I tried to parent them.

A FEW DAYS LATER, Allison and I went on a Christmas shopping trip together. Tommy wasn't with us. Allison and I both took advantage of the opportunity to talk candidly.

"Carl and I are thinking about a June 23rd wedding," Allison announced on the drive to the mall. I silently drove for a while, absorbing the information my brain didn't want to acknowledge.

On the drive back home, it was my turn. In my efforts to scare her with the permanence of marriage, I shared some mental-math with

Allison. "If you marry Carl this next summer, and live to be even as old as Grandma is, you'll have been married to Carl for almost sixty years! That's a really long time."

ALLISON SENT ME a text message from the basement the next afternoon. She was watching television.

"Brad wants to know if I can come for a visit Saturday."

Although Allison and Brad had been friends for several years, we usually only squeezed in a visit with him on weekends she visited Daniel.

Again, why are you going to visit another boy, Allison, if you're making plans to marry Carl in six months?

December 12th. Carl's rape case was supposed to be settled today. All Allison had talked about for the past month was how the case would be dismissed, just like the disseminating child pornography charges against *her* were dismissed in April. Several times during the day, I wanted to send Allison a text message asking if she heard anything yet, but I didn't. Finally, about 7:00 p.m., Allison came upstairs from the basement. "Carl's case has been postponed until January 30, 2012."

I asked Allison what that meant for her wedding plans.

"I don't know."

I had renewed hope the wedding would be postponed as well.

TWO DAYS LATER, wedding talk resumed. "Any church in town requires a minimum of two pre-marital counseling sessions," Allison's text message read at two in the afternoon.

I didn't respond. I had nothing to say.

Allison had another session with her therapist at three. She had been meeting with the therapist since July, as part of the follow-up care stemming from her legal troubles, and I always hoped the conversation with another adult would help Allison overcome her issues. Each visit, I sat in the waiting room, and looked forward to any morsel of information Allison might throw my way as we exited the building and drove back home.

I wasn't expecting what the therapist said as they walked out together. "It's time to go meet with the pastor."

What? Are you actually telling me you support Allison's insane marital plan?

"She called me just now," Allison said with a smile, "and asked if I'm free to visit with her, Mom. I told her we could be there in ten minutes."

"Oh!" was all I could manage to say, as I got up from the waiting room chair.

COULD ANYONE HAVE talked me out of marrying Frank?

I remember his friends constantly telling me what a loser Frank was, but I thought that was just guys teasing each other.

Two of the guys also made it perfectly clear they wished they could date me. I just needed to break it off with Frank, first.

THIRTEEN

CHRISTMAS VACATION ALLISON'S EIGHTEENTH BIRTHDAY

ALTHOUGH I KNEW it was nothing more than a temporary hiatus, I was thrilled when Christmas vacation began. I looked forward to ten days free from the drama of high school. Ironically, Allison substituted it with birthday and father drama.

I GREETED ALLISON on the morning of her eighteenth birthday by teasing her about not looking any different.

"I don't feel very different either," Allison replied.

The next day we drove to Chicago to spend Christmas with my sister. Allison wanted to see her dad as well.

We dropped Allison off at Frank's new place about nine in the morning, and he didn't even walk over to the car to greet his son. Tommy looked up briefly from the book he was reading in the back seat, made a quiet noise, and turned back to his book. Frank's loss, Tommy's pain.

The plan was to pick Allison up at noon. Her father had to be on the 12:30 p.m. "L" train for work. She called at 11:30 a.m. asking for more time. "Tammy and I are going to go shopping," Allison explained. Tammy was Frank's roommate. Frank's second wife no longer lived with him.

Was Tammy taking Allison for the much-desired birthday tattoo? I couldn't stop it from happening anymore, so I chose to focus on having holiday fun with Tommy and my sister instead.

By 2:00 p.m., my spirits were lightened. Allison sent me a text message saying, "Dad's being a douche."

Had the tattoo-dream had gone awry?

Had Frank finally disappointed Allison, too?

Rather than ask the questions I most wanted answered, I proceeded with caution. "Would you like a ride home now?" I sent back.

Allison's response didn't come until 2:26 p.m. "I don't know. Tammy and I are out shopping. I'm just annoyed with Dad."

How was Frank annoying Allison if he was at work, and she was with Tammy? The answer came at 3:18 p.m., in the form of a phone call from Allison.

"Dad wouldn't pay for my tattoo. I got my tongue pierced instead."

Lovely.

"He wouldn't even pay for it," Allison continued. "I know you don't like it, but it's not as permanent as a tattoo, at least."

Who taught you to rationalize your way through an argument so well?

But you punched a hole through the middle of your tongue for no other reason than you could—without my permission—because you are eighteen years and one day old.

We returned home to Minnesota after what felt like an eternity. I looked forward to unpacking the car, relaxing on the couch, eating dinner, and going to bed. Allison had other plans.

"I'm going to hang out with Matt," she said, practically running me over while I collected clothes to be laundered.

"Excuse me," I began. "I thought we were going to have dinner after I got this load started."

"I already ate," Allison threw back over her shoulder. "Love you!" and she was out the door.

When she returned two hours later, she headed straight to the shower. No "Hello," no, "I'm home," just straight into the shower.

An hour later, she was headed out the door again. "I just want to get away from you!" she screamed.

Thanks. I love you too, Allison.

Neither of us spoke when she returned home.

When Allison finally surfaced from her basement bedroom the next day (at 1:00 p.m.), she came right up to me for a hug. Allison's trademark way of apologizing without words. I hugged her back.

I DON'T REMEMBER hearing my parents ever apologize to me for anything. Was it just their generation's way? My father was born in 1924, my mother in 1936. Theirs was the generation that raised children to be seen and not heard, and viewed a child's questioning the parent as talking back. Would parents like that feel the need to apologize to a child for anything?

Frank never apologized, either. Everything was always *my* fault, according to him. I learned to live without receiving apologies from people.

That's why I was so moved when Officer Vic Richards apologized to me for not answering the phone when Allison and I returned to town in April 2009.

I WENT TO BED about 11:30 p.m. on December 30th—much later than I prefer, but I was trying to adjust my internal clock for New Year's Eve. At 12:58 a.m., Allison was sitting on the edge of my bed. "Can I go out with Katie? I'll be back before six."

"You mean six in the morning?" I asked in disbelief. I wasn't sure how long Allison had been sitting on the edge of my bed, or how much she had said before her question about going out.

"Okay, I'll be back in an hour," Allison replied.

Even though I'd just been woken from a pretty sound sleep, I couldn't find any logic in a jump from a 6:00 a.m. return time to a 2:00 a.m. return time. "No," was all I managed to say.

"But Mom . . ." Allison continued in her whiney voice—the one she had been using to get her way since she was a child.

"You're not going out at one o'clock in the morning," I said in my tersest, sleep-filled voice.

"We just want to watch a movie," Allison continued. "Since you won't let me go out tomorrow night, after I get done babysitting."

Babysitting for a family that lived on our block. Babysitting on New Year's Eve. Why *should* I let my eighteen-year-old daughter go out after midnight on New Year's Eve? While I felt my two statements were crystal clear, Allison wanted to continue bargaining.

"Well, at least I didn't sneak out. So can I go?"

"No!"

MY PARENTS' WORD was law. Unquestionable, unequivocal, non-negotiable law.

I don't think I wanted to be as tyrannical a parent as my parents had seemed, but I also have never understood why *everything* I said seemed negotiable to Allison.

IN SPITE of the middle-of-the-night interruption, I woke up the next morning hoping for a brighter day.

The first thing I noticed was the virgin layer of snow outside the front door. Allison hadn't exited through the front door, at least. There was no way to say if she left through any of the other exit points from our house, but I let it go for the sake of a good day.

By 1:30 p.m., the mantra began again. The day's snowfall cut the babysitting start time for the evening from 7:00 p.m. to 9:00 p.m., so Allison believed it would be an earlier end time than midnight. "So, can I go out with Katie tonight?"

"No."

I was thrilled when Allison sent me a text message at 11:40 p.m., telling me she was heading home from her babysitting job. I erroneously interpreted the message as a sign: the kids and I were going to watch the New Year's ball drop in Times Square like we had every other year. No sooner was Allison in the house, though, than she announced, "Katie's coming to get me."

"Excuse me?"

"We're going over to her house, remember? Since I didn't sneak out last night."

"I never said you could go."

"You can't stop me, either."

"Excuse me," I choked out. "This is my house, and you are still my daughter."

"So, I can just move out now."

Allison may have spat the words out, but they entered my heart like knives. "Then you won't have to put up with me anymore," she continued.

I wanted to slap Allison across her smart mouth. Instead, I walked into the bathroom.

"Mom, the ball's about to drop," Tommy yelled. When I didn't respond, he repeated, louder. "Mom, the ball's about to drop!"

When I still didn't respond, Tommy ran to the bathroom. Just in time, I managed to get the bathroom door locked—something I never do. "Mom, the ball's about to drop!"

"I heard you," was all I could say. What I couldn't explain was why I was no longer in the mood to celebrate.

From the peace of the bathroom, I sent Allison a text message at 12:08 a.m. "This house is not yours to run."

Receiving no rebuttal text message from her. I fooled myself into believing the fight was fizzling. Sadly, she was just waiting in the living room to spit more words into my face when I exited the bathroom.

"I just can't stand being here anymore," she yelled when I came out. "We're always fighting, and yesterday you were even yelling at Tommy for eating all of your bread!"

"That was very special bread . . ." I began, then realized she was just baiting me into a fight again. It's not a problem for Allison to yell at Tommy when he touches her iPod, or eats her candy, but it's apparently a problem when *I* yell at him for eating a half a loaf of expensive bread I bought in Chicago. Rather than take the bait, I returned to the bathroom to brush my teeth. At 12:12 a.m., I sent Allison one more text from the bathroom: "If you think you can avoid fighting in your life, I guess you're going to be living alone."

Once I finished in the bathroom, I walked out to the living room, kissed each child's head in turn, told them I loved them, and walked down the hall to my bedroom.

I heard the front door open and shut before the chill left the sheets.

I didn't know what to do anymore.

FOURTEEN

JANUARY—DEFIANCE

NEW YEAR'S DAY. My alarm clock woke me at 6:30 a.m.. Time for church. Tommy wanted to have a friend over after church. Rather than spoil their fun, I tried to be my cheery self, and waited for Allison in simmering silence.

Finally at 2:57 p.m., she sent me a text message. "I'm now awake enough to leave, but Katie isn't."

I toyed with my response. Should I tell her I thought her leaving without permission the night before meant she wasn't coming home anymore? Should I offer to drive over and pick her up? Should I ignore her, the way she ignores me?

By 3:53 p.m., I decided on a response. "At least I now know you are alive."

When the hands on the clock passed 5:00 p.m., and I hadn't received any more word from Allison, my anger began to boil. I sent a text message to my friend Sara at 5:13 p.m.: "Allison left home just after midnight last night, without permission, and she's still not home—grrrrr."

Since I didn't have Internet access at home, Sara filled me in on the Internet-front. "She's been on her social networking site—informing everyone of her New Year's cheer."

I *didn't have a New Year's cocktail, or watch the New Year's ball drop, but* she *spent the rest of the night drinking. Lovely.*

At 6:06 p.m., Allison sent her next text. "Katie will take me home when the movie is finished. We're more than halfway through it."

Just before 7:00 p.m., Allison walked through the front door. Once again, no "Hello," no "How are you?" just a direct walk to the bathroom. She showered, made herself a scrambled egg, brushed her teeth, and headed to bed.

Seventeen hours later, Allison resurfaced. She walked over to me, hugged me, and said, "I'm sorry."

"Sorry for what, specifically?" I asked. I wanted Allison to be clear and admit where she felt she went wrong.

"For going out the other night, and for calling you stupid."

I accepted her apology by giving her another hug. "How are we going to go forward?" I asked while still hugging.

I explained to Allison that living in my house meant living by my rules; she couldn't ignore my rules whenever she felt like it because Tommy was going to follow whatever example she set.

"I know. I'm sorry."

An hour later, Allison was outside, shoveling the driveway—by herself. I had planned on going out to shovel when the movie I was watching was over, but Allison didn't know that. I could not remember a time when Allison voluntarily shoveled the snow.

I'VE HEARD OF PARENTS who assign chores to their children as a form of punishment. I've never wanted chores to be seen as a punitive activity, because they felt that way to me as a child. My sister, four years older, got to dust and vacuum the living room every Saturday. I got to clean the only bathroom in our two bedroom apartment.

I also don't pay the children to do chores. In my opinion, things like laundry, cooking, cleaning, raking, and shoveling are part of being a member of a household. You can either watch me do them all, and hear me say, "No," when you ask for something like having a friend stay overnight, or a special item from the store—or you can help me, and reap the rewards of helping.

ALLISON RECEIVED a thick envelope in the mail January 3rd. I was excited to see a return address with the words *Admissions Office*. The envelope was from one of the out-of-state colleges Allison applied to before she began talking about wedding plans.

"Congratulations," Allison read the enclosed letter aloud. "You have been accepted . . ."

"Wonderful!" I cheered. "I'm so proud of you! And I have to admit, I'm a tiny bit jealous, too. I would love to teach there! But you got admitted! Good for you, sweetie. I'm so proud of you."

Will she go? I think having choices is the important thing. Perhaps she will stop thinking about getting married, knowing she has more options.

Driving her to the public library an hour later, Allison was on her cell phone. "I don't know. I'm either going to Montana (the college) or Wyoming (the marriage). I just have a lot to think about," I heard her tell the person on the phone.

I find hope in the smallest sentences.

An hour later, I worked up the nerve to ask Allison about the erasure of the wedding dress appointment on the calendar.

"Yeah," she began. "I told them I needed to postpone it. I told them I'd call them back when I had everything figured out."

I had no way of knowing what precipitated the cancellation of the appointment, and wasn't about to ask. Perhaps Carl got cold feet. Perhaps he had only been patronizing Allison's dreams of getting married, and had finally come clean.

Ultimately, I was content with the knowledge Allison cancelled the dress appointment and was thinking about her options.

I AGREED TO MARRY Frank because I felt option-less. Hans, my best friend had gotten married on my twenty-first birthday.

Even though Hans and I never dated, or even kissed, I internalized the movie message "I married my best friend" enough times during my life to believe *that* was the key to success. The *Brady Bunch*, *Partridge Family*, and *Jackson Five* were my peers. Buffy and Jody lived with a wonderful, loving uncle. Nancy Drew's dad never yelled when her natural inquisitiveness solved the mystery. Gloria ended up married to a great guy she met in college, in spite of Archie Bunker's awful behavior.

I was too young to understand my parents' miserable marriage was my dad's fault. I was too young to understand my father's volatile moods, low self-image, or drinking fueled the fire of his discontent.

I was too broken to understand I needed to find someone who *wasn't* just like my father.

When Hans married someone else, I worried about my own future. If my best friend didn't want me, I rationalized, who ever would?

THE MORNING of January 6th, the *Today* show aired their first here-she-is-again news story about Casey Anthony, the young mother from Florida who was freed from jail in July. "We've heard the word 'narcissist' thrown around a lot," I think I heard the reporter say. Hearing the words, "the definition of a sociopath . . . takes no responsibility for their actions," and "doesn't change their behavior even after being caught" gave me the chills. Those two descriptions seemed to fit Allison as well. *Is a sociopath created by the environment,* I wondered, *or is it something genetically predisposed, like addictive tendencies or body shape and size?*

Before I headed to work, I sent my friends Sara and Lindsey each a text message asking for their opinions about Allison being a sociopath. Then from work, I tried searching for the DSM-IV definition to satisfy my curiosity, but decided the answer might change the way I parented Allison the last months of her already difficult senior year. Could I, for instance, endure more fights with her about starting all over with another new psychiatrist? Could I take more time away from work—and attention from Tommy—to visit specialists in Fargo or Minneapolis? Therapists were always sending us away, after a few visits, saying Allison was "cured," or "fine," before they even offered to set up appointments for me. I didn't create Allison's behavior. I wasn't sleeping around, bringing a new guy home every week. I wasn't out at bars, ignoring my children for hours while I got drunk. I didn't walk away from being a parent, like Frank.

Although I'm only her mom, rather than a school-trained psychologist, psychiatrist, or social worker, Allison's behavior appeared to be getting worse over time. She'd been through court proceedings for running away, had been on ninety days of probation for shoplifting, and had spent nearly twenty-four hours in juvy for the pictures she emailed—yet she had a new digital camera in her dresser drawer two weeks before her eighteenth birthday. I found it while putting clean clothes away.

When we got home from school, Allison asked permission to have a new boy "hang out" at our house for a while. I thought this was very nice, considering most of her previous young men had remained faceless names. Allison talked about them, went to see movies with them, and even got rides home from school with them—but I was never allowed to meet them. Until Matt, who came to the house at 4:00 p.m.

Matt was a nice looking, clean-cut young man, tall, firm handshake, steady eye contact, bright smile. I was impressed with Allison's new friend. Although I still had lingering concerns regarding sociopathy from the morning, I clung to the hope Allison wouldn't become the major news story discussed some day.

I hoped, until I received Lindsey's reply. "I think she is a master at manipulation. She gets pleasure, or payback, for making you feel bad. It isn't good enough just to destroy herself, she wants to destroy you."

My heart dropped. *Does Allison really hate me that much?*

"So you think it's true? Or not?" I sent back. The question I was ultimately asking: Do you think Allison is a sociopath?

"I didn't used to," Lindsey replied, "but now I am starting to. Especially if she doesn't take ownership. If she feels her unhappiness is your fault. She will want you as unhappy as her."

It's hard to think about your child hating you so much she would purposely hurt you the way Lindsey suggested, but Frank manipulated me for so, so long. And if Frank was talking to Allison all the time, giving her additional information about how to manipulate people in general—and me specifically—there was no way to predict how far Allison's behavior would extend. One time, Allison mentioned her dad saying, "No one understands people like us." While I didn't understand the importance of the comment then, it still echoes back into my consciousness every so often.

No parent wants to think their child is capable of such intentional and focused hatred, but the careful manipulation of my feelings could be the payback Lindsey suggested, the payback for placing parental limits on her perception of a young adult's freedoms.

It must have been pre-school when someone first described Allison as being strong-willed.

I remember thinking it was a good characteristic. No one would be able to push my daughter around the way I had been pushed around. No one would be able to take advantage of my daughter the way so many had taken advantage of me.

When she played in the mud, wearing a cute pink outfit she had chosen, I cringed because I wondered how to get the mud out—not because Allison was in it.

When she flew through the air in a gymnastics class at five years old, I marveled at the courage Allison had. She must have practiced more than a hundred times to make the jump on the springboard, which propelled her over the vault, appear so effortless.

When I saw her for the first time in the waiting area of the psychiatric hospital in Chicago, after she ran away from home, I rushed across the room, tears streaming down my face, relieved that my daughter was whole—and safe.

Only *now* was I beginning to accept the fact Allison won't take "No" for an answer. If she heard "No" from me, she asked the next person—and the next person—until she heard "Yes."

But this was only the case for things Allison *wants*.

Allison came upstairs just before noon on January 7th. Matt called Allison. He wanted to "hang out" for a while. Allison was out the door by 1:00 p.m.

Matt dropped her back off about 4:00 p.m., and I started to think about what to make for dinner. Before I could flesh out the menu, though, Allison got a call from Katie. "Can I go out for pizza with Katie?"

Katie pulled into the driveway about 5:30 p.m., and Allison was out the door.

At 7:11 p.m., I received a text message from Allison. "Can I spend the night with Katie tonight, if I don't drink? She's all alone at her boyfriend's house, because he won't be here."

Rather than waste time arguing with Allison about the lack of logic to her inquiry, I simply replied with a "No" at 7:13 p.m.

"What time do I need to be home then?"

Rather than reply too quickly with a time I might later regret, I took a few minutes to think about my answer. "Before I go to bed," I sent back at 7:18 p.m.

"So like 10:30 p.m.?"

"That would be livable."

Allison came home at 10:35 p.m., loudly announcing, "I'm home on time!" as she shut the front door behind her.

I REMEMBER WORKING really hard to hide my experimentation with smoking and drinking from my parents.

When I was in eighth grade, I liked a boy who happened to smoke. Rather than be made fun of for one more thing, I would sneak a few cigarettes from my dad's pack every so often. But, in order to not be caught, I would wait to light up until I was on an "L" train platform—or walk through an alley in my neighborhood, rather than the street—so no parents would see me.

Drinking at seventeen took on the same level of sneakiness.

So why does Allison so blatantly announce what *she* does? Is she hoping I'll make a big deal out of it? Or, is she hoping Frank will? (He's one of the many Friends on her social networking site.)

Allison wore a skirt to school January 13th, a barely-covers-your-behind skirt, without nylons or tights for warmth, in spite of a temperature forecast in the high single digits.

"Can I hang out with Katie?" she asked me when she reached the car after school. *How about a hello, how are you, thanks for picking me up from school today, Mom?*

Rather than start the fight at the curb, I simply said, "Why don't we go home first, so you can put on warmer clothes."

"Katie, can you pick me up at home? I'm going to put on some pants real quick," Allison said into her cell phone.

They left the house at three-thirty. "I'll be home by six," Allison shouted over her shoulder as she stepped out the front door

Just before seven, Allison called. "Can I stay over at Katie's house for a while? We're going to watch a movie. Her mom said, 'We haven't seen Allison for a while, Katie. Why doesn't she join us for Family Movie Night?'"

Allison didn't get home until 1:28 a.m. The first door bell woke me up. The second had me focused and climbing out of bed. The third was just annoying, as I was walking down the hall towards the living room.

"Thanks for calling to let me know anything," I said as Allison walked through the front door.

"Sorry," Allison began, "but my battery ran out at eight."

"And there are no other phones on the planet," I grumbled as I headed back towards my bedroom—and sleep.

Allison came upstairs the next morning at 11:00 a.m. I had expected her to sleep until noon or one o'clock in the afternoon. Being awake at eleven meant someone called her and invited her out again.

"Katie and I are going to go out for coffee," were the first words out of her mouth. No mention of the early-morning arrival, no apology for staying out so late, no lift at the end of the sentence, to imply I was being asked for permission.

Twenty minutes after she left, Allison sent a text—asking permission. "Can I spend the night with Katie tonight? I will bring my English homework. She needs help with her math."

Sure. You haven't taken math since last year—but she needs your help with her math. How stupid do you think I am, Allison.

Allison returned home unexpectedly at two, and headed downstairs. An hour later, I heard a loud bang coming from somewhere within the house, and yelled down the stairs, "What was that?"

Allison came upstairs to give her answer. "I don't know, I thought it was from upstairs."

While I walked to the front door to look out, Allison ran to the back corner of the house—to her brother's bedroom window. My suspicions were raised even more. I proceeded with what I then felt was a futile examination of the house, because I wanted Allison to understand I am always on guard duty.

When I got to Allison's room, I was rewarded. Her bedroom window was unlocked, open a tiny bit, and the blind was all twisted and turned. I decided to keep a close eye on the window going forward.

TELEVISION SHOWS and movies show kids sneaking out of their bedroom windows all the time. When we lived in Wyoming, and Allison had the bedroom in the basement, she once told me how Carl got crabby because her window had a screen he couldn't remove without cutting it. I was annoyed to hear he had investigated the possibility, but was thrilled to hear it was impossible.

Unfortunately, the basement bedroom window in *this* house was much easier to exit. I watched Allison and a neighbor's grandson climb out of her bedroom window, in fact, during one of the previous summer's block parties held on the empty lot next to our house.

I grew up in the second floor apartment of a walk-up apartment building in Chicago from the time I was seven until I moved out as a wife at twenty-one. The only way I could have ever escaped through a window in the apartment would have been if a firemen's hook-and-ladder truck was waiting.

JANUARY 16TH. Allison sent me a text message from Katie's house shortly after midnight last night. I received it when I turned my phone on this morning. "Someone hacked into Jeremy's profile and is stalking me through my phone and my social networking site."

The first response to go through my head was, *Duh! You play around with strangers on the Internet—do you really think they're all nice and wholesome people, with only the best of intentions?*

According to her social networking site, Allison spent a lot of time talking with people via an Internet live-chat program. Was she talking to people she knew? Or was she making new acquaintances through technology? The latter thought scared me the most. Meeting new people via technology was what got her on the bus at fifteen. Going to the police with my concerns didn't seem like a good idea, though, considering the history Allison already had with the local authorities. Would they merely criminalize her behavior like last time, rather than help her change or make better choices?

The second response in my head was, *What do you expect me to do about it? You don't even want to live in my house anymore—how can you come back whining to me when things don't turn out the way you want them to?*

Allison was constantly with Katie—"spending the night," with brief stops at home to change clothes. She came home from the New Year's Eve celebration with a hickey on her neck. She told her brother she didn't know who did it, or when it got there. What else couldn't she remember?

The third response was, *Why can't you just be honest with me, for once, and take responsibility for your own actions? No one hacked into Jeremy's profile. I'll bet dollars to donuts you gave your information out to the wrong guy again, and now you regret it!*

The fourth response: *Gee, too bad you haven't learned from the five other times I've paid to change your phone number. Wonder when you'll have enough babysitting money saved up to pay me to change your phone number this time.*

Rather than begin her day with a fight, I simply sent back the response "Wow" at 6:50 a.m.

Is there a way to help a child who's unwilling to see her behavior as risky?

I sent Allison a text message at 10:15 a.m., to remind her of the afternoon appointment with the counselor. "I will leave work at 1:30 p.m., and whip home to pick you up for your appointment," working from the assumption Katie would be dropping her off at our house that morning.

"Katie is going to bring me," Allison replied.

"So I'll meet you there?"

"I was going to hang out with her," Allison sent back.

"You have been," I replied. *For several days, in fact. Without my permission.*

As though she read my mind, rather than the three-word text, Allison sent a final message at 10:20 a.m.: "I'm moving out Tuesday."

Tuesday.

As in, tomorrow? Or, Tuesday of next week?

My mind reeled. I knew she was eighteen, which meant the law took away my parental controls. I also thought we had an agreement. I thought Allison was going to stay home until her graduation. We had ordered the cap, gown, and graduation announcements. We had talked about the graduation party. We had agreed I would drive her wherever she wanted to go—the day after graduation. But with a single text message, Allison was threatening to take it all away.

At 1:18 p.m., Allison sent me a text message. "On my way. Got my period, so I'll be going home to get my clothes and backpack after the appointment."

As I drove up to the therapist's building, I started to feel the rising levels of anxiety I felt when I headed into the courthouse in

April 1998, to dissolve my marriage with Frank. For me, Allison's text messaged plan for emancipation felt just like Frank's.

Allison: "I'm still going to live in town for a while," she explained to the counselor, "then in February, I'll move to Wyoming."

Frank: "I'm just going to move out for a while, and let you straighten everything out."

Frank's definition of everything: the kids, the finances, my behavior towards him.

Frank moved back to Chicago when my attorney served him with the divorce papers.

The counselor asked Allison questions designed to make her think: "Will doing that help you, Allison? Then, why do it?" and "What might be a better alternative than that?"

Unfortunately, Allison wouldn't budge. "I just can't take it anymore," she nearly screamed, while starting to cry. "My mom and brother are yelling at me all of the time, putting me down—I just can't take it anymore."

Just like Frank, everything wrong in Allison's life was someone else's doing. Frank couldn't keep a job for more than six months or a year, because someone hassled him. Allison couldn't get a job because everyone in town hated her. Never mind that neither Allison nor Frank could receive constructive criticism. Never mind that Allison only helped with chores around the house when she wanted me to buy her something. Never mind that Allison was annoyed by every little sound (or smell) her brother produced . . . Never mind that Frank didn't pay the court-ordered child support.

"If we just move to a different place," Frank repeatedly cooed, "we will have more money."

If I had just listened, and done what I was told, everything would have been fine.

The counselor took on the mediator role. "You need to have some conversation with your mom, Allison, if you want to handle this like an adult. The two of you need to work out things like whether or not you still get to have a house key, what happens to your cell phone line, the terms for coming over for a visit, and whether or not you can spend the night when you come over for those visits.

"Does your mom even have contact information for you, in case she needs to get a hold of you for anything? Who are you staying with? Have you given your mom the address and phone number for that family?"

That's when Allison took it up a notch. "You have to understand, I can't tell my mom anything. When I do, she just freaks out."

"Allison," the counselor said in the tone of voice adults use when they are addressing a child who is projecting the blame, "your mom is sitting right here. She wouldn't be here if she didn't care."

"Oh, yeah? How about the time she hit me."

"Allison," I said rather sharply. "That was *one* time."

"Whatever, Mom. You scarred me for life when you hit me."

"Are you saying you're afraid of your mom?" the counselor asked in what seemed like a disbelieving tone.

"Allison, how many times are you going to bring that up?" I said, angry and annoyed. "That was when you were thirteen years old, and you were inviting a predator to our house!"

"But you hit me in the head, Mom!"

"Upside the back of your head, Allison." Not that I was trying to diminish what I had done, I just didn't want the counselor to think I had punched Allison in the face or something.

"You could have hit me anywhere else, Mom," Allison bit out, through the tears.

"No, I was driving. You'd screamed at me, plugged your headphones into your ears the way you do when you want to shut everyone out, and had physically turned your body to face the passenger window. I just wanted to—" *get your attention, knock some sense into your head, smack you across the mouth for swearing at me—I don't remember anymore. But you sure remember, Allison. You bring it up whenever you want to shut me down. Or, perhaps you're hoping to get me arrested. I don't know anymore. But it sure as hell hurts that you can hang onto something that happened five years ago, and shove it back into my face whenever you please.*

I explained to the counselor why this act-of-emancipation was so difficult for me. "It's just that through all of her court stuff and everything, everyone has been so concerned with my knowing exactly where Allison is at every moment, what she's doing on the Internet, how she got the camera she used, why she's talking to men she doesn't know. All of this time, I'm held totally accountable and responsible for everything she does, and now I'm just supposed to let go because she turned eighteen?"

"I know it's been harder for you than for most parents," the counselor began, "but that's the way foster parents feel too . . ."

I tuned out some of the rest of her explanation, because I didn't see how she could compare the experiences and feelings a birth mother has for her child to that of a foster parent. What mattered for me was the bottom line: Allison was allowed to do whatever she wanted, just because she passed some stupid, arbitrary birthday.

In spite of how she talked to me in the counselor's office, Allison left the building with me, hugged me in front of my car, then walked over to Katie's car.

Fifteen minutes after I got home, Allison was ringing the front door bell. "I'm here to get some of my things," she said, as Katie followed her into the house.

The girls only stayed for fifteen minutes. Allison left, carrying out a canvas bag of clothes and a pair or two of shoes. "I love you, Mom," she said before she shut the door behind her.

I love you too, dear.

Twenty-four hours later, I still didn't have my house key back, I still didn't have a name or address for the people with whom Allison was staying, I still didn't have peace of mind about Allison's health and well-being. What I *did* have was a basket with her dirty clothes, her unmade bed, and a deep sadness in my heart.

I CAN ALMOST count the number of times I didn't sleep in my own home on the fingers of my two hands.

1) The time my dad got "sick" when I was ten. We were staying at my grandmother's house in Minnesota when my mom got the call from the hospital. My mom left my sister and me there, while she returned to Chicago for the surgery to repair the damage caused by the bursting of the cranial aneurysm,

2) Girl Scout camping trips,

3) The trip I took with my best friend and her family to Tennessee when I was in seventh grade,

4) The time my dad went down the hall of our apartment to get his hammer—so he could break my bedroom door down. I was seventeen, and feared for my life. I stayed at my best friend's house while my mother moved my dad to a nursing home,

5) The weekend trip I took with another friend and her family to Door County, Wisconsin, when we were eighteen,

6) The weekend trip I took with Rolf, when I was twenty, to pick Frank up from basic training in Virginia,

7) The night Frank and I eloped.

Perhaps I was an unusual child, because I never felt a need to leave home. Perhaps Allison's strong-willed nature allows her to do things many of us are too afraid to do.

THE SECOND DAY after Allison left, I received a text message right before noon. "Because of the cold weather, school may be cancelled tomorrow."

Okay. And you're telling me this, why?

The reason for the text message came two hours later. "Mom, you need to call the school, to let them know I'm no longer living at home."

I took a really long pause before speaking. "Why?"

"For the contact information stuff."

I took an even longer pause. "I need to find out about things like that, dear."

"What do you mean, Mom?"

I mean, dear, I'm hoping this act-of-emancipation isn't as final as you are making it sound. I mean, dear, I still want to get the email notifications when you are absent from school. I still want to receive your grades (which will be sent out next week). I still want to think you're coming back home next week, or the week after.

Allison didn't like the prolonged silence. "Like, for calling me out of school and stuff, Mom."

And that's what the phone call is all about, isn't it, Allison. You are now standing in the attendance office, wanting to skip your last class of the day, and they won't let you go without your parent's permission.

When I didn't agree to do it, Allison hung up the phone.

By four-thirty, a different version of Allison surfaced, via text message: "Is it okay if I stop by before 7:00 to get clothes?"

I sent back a simple, "Yep."

Ten minutes later, another text. "If you ever want me over to talk, or for dinner, I'd be glad to. Should I do laundry somewhere else?"

"You can do it here, if you stay and visit." *I'm not a drop-off laundry facility. If you do only one load of laundry, that gives me about thirty minutes to wash, and thirty or more minutes to dry. I can manage to say a lot in an hour.*

"Oh. Katie has to be home by 7:00," Allison replied. "Is 6:30 okay?"

So, Katie has rules she follows. Even though Katie has been eighteen longer than you, Allison, and has her own car, she still follows her parents' rules. I hope this time living with her shows you something.

When Allison rang the doorbell at 6:45 p.m., I smiled. When she came into the house alone, without Katie following behind, I was thrilled. I was in the middle of making dinner, and had been thinking about the possibility of Allison sitting down with us at the dinner table again—something I had been missing since she began staying at Katie's house so much. Ten minutes later, she was carrying her bags back towards the front door. She had merely exchanged dirty clothes for clean, thanks to the surplus of clothes in her dresser.

"Oh, I thought you were doing laundry tonight," I said, trying to keep the disappointment out of my voice.

"No, Katie has to be home at seven."

A quick glance at the kitchen clock revealed it was already 7:04 p.m. Again, I couldn't help but find the irony: when I told Allison she needed to be home by 9:30 p.m. on a school night, she accused me of treating her like a five-year-old. But when Katie needed to be home by 7:00 p.m., it was a statement of fact, to be honored.

JANUARY 19TH. Allison had been gone three days. At 6:47 p.m., Allison sent me a text message requesting help, although she never formally asked. "Well, after school tomorrow I have no where to stay. Cheyenne's boyfriend dumped her so she isn't texting me."

"I'm sure your mom would take you," I typed into my cell phone, "but you didn't want to live in her house with her rules . . ."

It took Allison an hour to reply. "I'm willing to work something out."

"With whom?"

"You and I."

Not wanting to be taken advantage of, I wanted to make sure we nailed down some terms and conditions. I didn't want to have the discussion over text messaging, though. I asked Allison if she wanted to talk in person.

"When?"

"I'm home now/tonight—or tomorrow after 1:30 p.m."

"Tomorrow. Katie can't leave tonight."

Once again, you're both willing to honor Katie's parents' rules, which happen to align with so many of my own rules, but you won't honor mine. Wow. That speaks volumes, Allison.

"Okay—or call the house phone tonight. You can decide what works best for you."

"All right. When I finish my homework, I'll call."

Homework? Allison is doing her homework before ten o'clock at night? I would really like to meet Katie's parents!

Or maybe I don't. What kind of garbage have you been telling them about me this past week? Katie's parents must think I'm absolutely horrible.

Allison called the house at 9:15 p.m. We talked for nearly a half hour, discussing the issues bothering each of us.

1) Allison: "I just don't like the way you expect me to be home at 9:30 p.m. It makes me feel like I'm five years old."

Me: "I'm sorry, dear, but it's just my having grown up in Chicago. I can't go to bed until I've made sure all of the doors are locked. If you are out, I can't go to bed. If I can't go to bed, I don't get enough sleep, and then it makes me tired and crabby the whole next day—which becomes a vicious cycle for the week. It's different when you are babysitting, because I know you are somewhere safe, doing a job. But, when you are just 'out,' I worry about you getting into a car accident, or so many other things that could go wrong."

Allison: "Mom, we live in a small town."

Me: "I understand that, dear. But I didn't grow up in a small town, and I didn't have a nice, safe childhood."

2) Allison: "I wish you would stop treating me like a child. I'm eighteen now. My friends get so much more freedom than you give me."

Me: "Well, if you were to help out more around the house, rather than lie around on the couch all of the time and watch TV, I might be able to think of you as an adult."

Allison: "But I do help out."

Me: "Once a month isn't enough, though. I'm talking about doing something every single day. Every day, I'm cooking, washing clothes, washing dishes, or cleaning the house. I get frustrated when you're just lounging on the couch, or running out with your friends. If you helped out, and did something every single day, I'd see you more as an adult."

By the time we hung up, we had agreed Allison would come home with me after school the next day.

Allison sent me a text message at 11:11 a.m.: "Can I hang out with Katie a bit after school? Then she'll drop me off at the house with my stuff. It'll be easier than transferring it in the school parking lot."

I felt wedged between a rock and a hard place again. If I said no, I feared Allison would take it as a sign that I'm forever inflexible, and would never come home. But if I said yes, I feared becoming a push-over. I had to decide which was more important.

At 4:43 p.m., Allison began the next round of negotiations: "Can Katie come over for dinner?"

Katie stayed until the ten o'clock news began.

I REMEMBER BEING alone most of the time during my senior year of high school. My sister was in her senior year of college in South Dakota. My dad was in the nursing home, and my mom was working three jobs and spending time at the nursing home with my dad when she got done with work on the weekends.

All I wanted, at that age, was to have someone in the apartment I could talk to, and eat meals with.

Now I own my own home. I still sadly find myself eating too many meals alone, and/or in silence.

JANUARY 24TH, another flimsy Allison excuse for hanging out with Katie all night: "Doing homework. Helping Katie with chem."

Right. Have you ever even taken chemistry, Allison? I know you took biology in tenth grade, and forensic science the first part of this year or the latter part of last year, but chemistry? I don't think you're telling me the truth, dear.

Allison came home at 11:30 p.m., on a school night. She had been drinking, based on the glass of chocolate milk and bowl of scrambled eggs she consumed before heading off to bed.

January 25th, my friend Lindsey sent a text message about Allison's apparent new boyfriend, based on information Allison posted on her social networking site. "She says she's in a relationship—with a boy from town. His name is Kaleb Strong. He will be twenty-one in April. He works at the mall in town." Lindsey also had information about his family, and described his profile picture.

So the June wedding to Carl in Wyoming is off?

January 26th, Allison was a hung-over, angry bear. She got home at 1:20 a.m., and woke her brother with a text message asking to be let in. I thought about letting her sleep in, and miss the day of school as punishment, but realized going to school with only five hours of sleep—and a hangover—would be a better punishment. I woke Allison up at seven to get ready for school, *after* I took the house key out of her purse.

The first time Allison ignored my curfew this week, I gave her the benefit of the doubt. I hoped her coming in at 11:30 p.m. was an honest mistake. I'm not so old I don't remember what having fun with your friends, and forgetting about the time is like at eighteen. But two nights in a row, and two hours later this time than the last time, I saw the blatant disregard behind the behavior.

I couldn't help but chuckle when she collapsed in the middle of drying her hair. Rather than stand up in the bathroom, Allison was blow drying her hair from a sitting position on the living room floor. One minute she was sitting upright, the next minute she was lying on her left side, blow dryer in her left hand, and brush in her right. I wanted to ask her how *that* was working for her, *a la* Dr. Phil McGraw, but chose to just chuckle to myself.

As the kids got out of the car at the high school, I gave my usual, "Love you! Have a good day! I'll be back to pick you up at . . ." cheer.

Allison responded with a grumbled, "Whatever, Mom. Shut up already," before slamming the car door.

Later in the day, I sent Allison a heart-felt text message: "You are always going to be my daughter. You are always going to be in my heart. If you ignore boundaries, like curfew, 'because I'm eighteen,' then we (Tommy and I) have the right to refuse to get out of bed and open the door for you, *etc.*"

January 27th, the kids and I drove to my mother's for a weekend's change of scenery. The next morning, Allison met Katie at a wedding dress shop. Katie was getting a new prom dress. Thirty minutes after dropping her off, Allison called me. "I found the perfect dress," she began. "It's the exact one I want!"

"You have a dress, Allison. I'm not buying you another one."

"It's only four hundred dollars, Mom."

After sputtering in the direction of the phone, I said, "No."

"But Mom . . ."

"No, dear. There's no way I'm paying for another expensive prom dress."

"But it's . . ."

Honestly, there was nothing Allison could say to secure her that particular dress—but she wouldn't let go of the idea.

"Honey, there's no way I can buy it."

Hearing those words, Allison hung up.

And then she sent me a text message: "With 20% off it's $360.00, and all you have to pay is $120.00 today."

All I have to pay. Today. Excuse me, dear, but why don't you get a job and pay for it yourself?

Four hours later, the child who had no visible means of income sent me a text message: "Got two piercings. Giving you a heads-up."

Three hours after receiving the text, I got to see the two new facial piercings—and the three bags of new clothes. "How did you get this stuff?"

"Oh, Benjamin gave me some money. When he found out I was going to the mall, and had no money, he gave me fifty dollars."

"Excuse me? He just gave you fifty dollars?"

"Yeah. He got like five hundred for . . . (I couldn't hear), so he gave it to me!" Allison cheerily explained.

I had flashbacks to her explanation of Gregory's dad giving her twenty-five dollars when she was running away. My head started to spin, and I started to get nauseous by the thoughts swirling around in my brain. But, I said nothing.

Allison and I apparently have a different moral code about what's right and what's wrong, but she's always going to be my daughter.

I STOLE A CANDY BAR from the corner store when I was thirteen years old. I didn't have any money, and was really, really hungry for that candy bar.

Shortly after that, we talked about the Ten Commandments at school. Number 7 in the Lutheran faith is "Thou Shalt Not Steal."

I felt terrible about the candy bar. I hadn't been starving. I just wanted the candy bar. I was afraid I would be banished to Hell for stealing one dumb candy bar.

Fear is what keeps me from thinking about stealing, to this day.

WE RETURNED HOME January 29th about five. Allison hurriedly helped unload the car and trunk, then immediately ran out the front door. "Katie's here," she yelled over her shoulder before shutting the front door.

Tommy stayed up playing his new video game long after I went to bed. At midnight, I remember him talking to me about losing track of the time. "Is she home yet?" I asked, rising up through the layers of sleep.

"No. Which one of us is going to let her in?" Tommy asked.

"Oh, go to bed, dear. She's not your responsibility. Thank you, but I've had enough of this nonsense. Tonight, she's going to find her angry mother on the other side of the door."

"Okay. Should I leave the living room light on?"

"No. Go ahead and turn it off, dear."

The doorbell rang at 12:20 a.m. I climbed out of bed, walked to the living room, and saw Allison huddled up between the front door and the screen door. (Our front door was half window.)

"I can't find my key," Allison said from her side of the door.

I just stood on my side, with my arms crossed.

"C'mon, Mom. My fingers are freezing."

I noticed the shaking of her arms. I noticed the hands tucked into the sweatshirt sleeves. I noticed the wetness of her eyes. I noticed the tone of impatience in her voice. "What time is curfew?" I asked in my steeliest voice.

Allison broke eye-contact, looking down towards her feet, before getting a new surge of adrenalin. "Are you serious? Let me in, please."

"Why should I?" I asked rhetorically, while unlocking the dead-bolt.

"I can just move out," Allison threw at me, with spite.

"This isn't a hotel, where you can just come and go as you please," I bit back at Allison while unlocking and opening the door.

She came in, moved quickly past me, and headed downstairs.

I returned to bed. Five minutes later, Allison quietly came back upstairs, and brushed her teeth.

Thirteen hours later, Allison sent a text message from school: "Can I hang out with Katie today? She needs help on her taxes."

Sure. You, who have no job, and have never filed an income tax return, are going to be able to help Katie with her taxes. If you are going to insist on lying to me, Allison, please come up with more realistic lies. Otherwise, you're really only adding insult to injury, by suggesting I'm stupid enough to believe your lame lies.

"When?" was all I sent back.

"After school."

"Be home by 9:30 p.m.—and understand that I'm not going to wash your clothes if all you are doing is sleeping here."

"Okay," she sent back twenty minutes later.

IT WAS REALLY HARD for me to accept this treatment from Allison. Part of me understood my role in creating her, though. For more years than I can remember, my mother had been preaching the message that I will have to clean up whatever messes Allison makes. "All you need is for her to get pregnant," my mother would say. Or, "You can't have her doing that!" There were even emails about how high school students are able to leave high school with as much as two year's worth of college credits under their belts. These were the tapes that ran over and over in my head. I was responsible for whatever Allison or Tommy did. I was responsible for providing them with food, shelter, and an education. I did not need to have my own friendships, or a new relationship with a man who might give Allison and Tommy the male support for which they yearned. I was supposed to take care of everything, no matter what.

I'm tired, Mom.

I'm tired, Allison.

I'm broke, Frank. Where's my court-ordered child support? I've had two jobs for more years than you've had one, and I still can't make enough to make the ends meet.

I'm weak, God. I need a support system to help hold me up. A few girlfriends would be nice. A man who loves me for who I am would be amazing. An intervention for Allison, to straighten her out before it's too late would be awesome. Hard to watch, but, I'm afraid, getting to the point of being necessary. Tommy tells me she's having sex with boys—in my house, while I'm even home. Apparently, Allison brags to Tommy about her various exploits. And now there is the issue of magically appearing money. Is she getting paid for pictures of herself again? Or, is she getting paid for performing sexual acts? I don't know that I want to know, so much as I want it stopped for Allison's sake.

FIFTEEN

FEBRUARY—ON THE MOVE

MY ALARM WOKE ME at 5:30 a.m. February 1st. *Did Allison come home? I don't remember getting up and letting her in . . .*

I checked the living room for her jacket, the front door rug for her shoes, the outside steps for footprints, and finally her bedroom.

I had gotten so used to her coming home in the middle of the night and spending unscheduled numbers of nights with Katie, I didn't recognize *real* moving out at first.

JUST BEFORE 10:00 A.M., Allison sent me a text message. "I need nine dollars for choir shirt for tomorrow," was all it said. No "good morning," no "I love you," no "sorry if I worried you last night." All she wanted was money.

I couldn't respond. I didn't know what to say. On the one hand, her choosing not to come home screamed, "I am an adult, and I don't need you anymore." I didn't want to give her any more money. She could get money from people for clothes and facial piercings—let them pay for her choir t-shirt as well.

On the other hand, this was a school uniform requirement. Every spring, the choir director had a different t-shirt design for each choir to wear for the Pop Concert. The year before, Allison got the t-shirt, but wasn't able to sing in the concert because the police had taken her to juvy. I was afraid my refusal to pay for the t-shirt this year would be an excuse for Allison to not participate in the choir concert. If she didn't participate, she could fail the class. If she failed the class, she might drop out of school. I didn't want to push my luck. And, it was only nine dollars.

Finally, at 11:41 a.m., I sent a reply. "School uniform requirement—I will pay it."

I expected a thank you text, but received nothing. Fifteen minutes later, I sent Allison another text. "Who do I make the check out to?"

Two minutes after four o'clock, Allison sent a text asking, "Can I stop by a little later? My phone is dying."

Allison rang the front door bell at 4:50 p.m. I smiled, unlocked the door, opened it, and watched Katie follow Allison in.

I followed Allison to her room, where she opened dresser drawers to pull out clean clothes for her suitcase. "Did you bring Katie as a buffer, then, so we can't talk?"

"We can talk, Mom."

"No, we can't, dear."

"Whatever."

I walked out to the kitchen to wait. From there, I watched Katie walk into Allison's room. I watched Allison sort through the bags she left beside the kitchen table three nights earlier. I watched Allison place clean clothes into the suitcase. When Allison came to the kitchen, though, and opened the refrigerator with her back to me, I lost my patience.

"You can't come in here and just raid for food if you're not staying," I said in a calm, but frustrated tone of voice.

"Whatever," was Allison's response as she slammed the refrigerator door. "I'll get some food somewhere else."

"You could eat here, dear, if you stayed to talk to me—but you brought Katie as a buffer, so we can't talk." I didn't care anymore if Katie heard me. She needed to know how upset the game made me.

"We did talk, Mom, at the therapist's that day."

"But, we're not having the conversation she said we need to be having at this point. The conversation where we talk about how this works. You still haven't provided me with the information about where you are staying, so I can get hold of you if I need to. That's how you would make this a mature moving out."

"Oh, so now you're calling me immature? Whatever. I can't stand living here anymore, Mom."

"So let's talk about it."

"I don't want to be yelled at, Mom."

"Am I yelling? No. I'm talking, dear."

"No you're not. You're yelling at me."

I wanted to ask Katie if it sounded like I was yelling, but she was too busy looking down at the floor, putting on her boots, and opening up the front door for Allison.

Just like that, Allison was gone again, after only five minutes at home.

I DON'T KNOW when I realized Allison moved out—she had been staying at Katie's house so much of January, threatening me with moving out every time I said something she didn't like, and sending me text messages I didn't always understand, like the one about not being able to stay at Charlene's anymore—but by the morning of February 8th I began reconciling myself to Allison's behavior. The text message I sent to my two closest friends read: "Maybe her moving out is a good sign, as it means she can't manipulate me."

My subconscious recognized the manipulation before my conscious was willing to accept it, because I remember the word coming out of my mouth while speaking to Officer Richards in April of 2009. I wanted to dismiss the possibility, because no parent wants to believe their own child is capable, much less *willing* to intentionally manipulate them. By this point, though, I realized I needed to love myself as much as I loved Allison. If Allison was so willing to hurt me, I needed to protect myself from her attacks to my emotions and fears. If Allison wanted to live somewhere else, I needed to let her go.

My friend Sara sent back the quickest response. "So true," her message began. "Though I think she will forever manipulate you and anyone around her. That's part of who she is."

Part of who she is. In her D.N.A. Hard-wired, not learned. Nature, not Nurture. Allison got this part from her dad. Frank is a master manipulator. That's why I was convinced to marry him so many years ago, how he was able to trick the system into giving him a reduction in child support every time he asked—money he never intends to pay—why he'd been bouncing from apartment to apartment (and roommate to roommate) since he moved out of our home in 1997. It was all just part of who Allison was.

Lindsey's reply came next. "I think that would be a positive thing if she couldn't manipulate you. She also needed to know what moving out and not having mom to pick up the pieces and buy things is like."

On the drive to the high school that morning, I told Tommy how important he would be to me in the later years, "when we're all old."

"It will be important for you to point out things, like when you think Allison is manipulating me, because she will. It will be, 'Mom, I need some money for . . . ,' or 'Mom, I really need somewhere to stay . . . ,' 'Mom, if only you could co-sign for . . . ,' or 'Mom, we just need to borrow . . .' I'll need you to point out those things, because I'll want to help her. I'll want to think this time it'll be different. I'll end up getting sucked back in, because I love her. So, you'll be there to tell me things, to remind me of how many other times, to take care of me, just like I'm now taking care of Grandma, okay?"

Tommy sat in silence until we got to the high school. "I love you, Mom," he said as he got out of the car.

I didn't mean to burden my sixteen-year-old son so early in the morning, but I was feeling too alone and vulnerable again.

Two hours after I dropped Tommy off at school, Lindsey sent another text: "Hang tough, my friend."

"Thanks," I sent back. "It's obviously hard. I walk around like a zombie most days—and function even less than that on non-work days."

"Time to focus on you," came Lindsey's response.

Great advice, but how? How do I focus on me, *all of the sudden, when the past fifteen years of my life have been almost exclusively focused on my role as a single mother, and taking care of my two children? I lost track of myself along the way.*

After work, I headed home. The house was empty. Tommy had another after-school practice. I decided I needed a project on which to focus my time and energy. But, what kind of project?

I could work on my taxes . . .

I decided to tackle Allison's room instead. Before she came home again, and started packing up or throwing everything out, I wanted to look for clues to help me figure out what she was doing, and how she was thinking. Clues I found in her room helped so much when she ran away in 2009.

Once again, I found more than I wanted to see. First, there was the empty pop can in the back of her closet. All of the times she told me Tommy was stealing my pop, it might have been Allison. Once I removed the pop can, I spotted the empty alcohol bottle. Another one of the hard lemonades I suspected were missing from the six-pack container above the refrigerator. Another of Allison's lies. She claimed Tommy was stealing those as well.

The information in her discarded notebooks was more difficult, though. One was from Wyoming, and revealed the sexually focused thoughts she had about two different boys she went to school with. Allison had been friends with each boy's sister. She had questioned the bi-sexuality of one boy, and contemplated the penis size of the other. These were not thoughts I remember having as a twelve- or thirteen-year-old girl. For reasons I may never understand, Allison was already focused on sex as a "tween."

I wanted to cry.

I wanted to throw up.

I went back upstairs.

I REMEMBER BEING called a *prude* when I was a teenager. Boys in the neighborhood wanted to find dark corners in alleys. Kissing them was fine, but when they wanted more . . . I heard the taunts as I walked away.

I heard the taunts repeatedly, for days and weeks after, until I learned to re-route the paths I took to the store, home from school, or to the bus stop.

I couldn't understand why "saving yourself" was viewed in such opposite ways. My Lutheran school upbringing told us to reserve it for the sanctity of marriage. My dad called me a slut because he caught me kissing my boyfriend good-bye on the back porch one day. Kids in my neighborhood called me a prude because I wouldn't let them touch me anywhere under my clothes.

FEBRUARY 11TH, I woke up to discover a text Allison sent me after I turned off my phone the night before. "Can I come by tomorrow for my towel?"

"Which towel?" I sent back after reading the message. "Want me to put it out for you, in case we are running errands?"

"Well, I made a little list," Allison replied. "Like I need my towel, and a dishcloth to wash dishes with, and body wash."

"Run over now?" I offered.

"Okay. It'll have to be a kind of quick drop in, because the car doesn't have heat."

Oh, my goodness. What kind of life have you created for yourself, Allison? You are with someone who drives a car without heat, and you are coming home to get supplies for living somewhere else? I just don't understand.

When I opened the door, I discovered a disheveled, yet-to-shower young woman who faintly resembled my daughter. The smell of stale cigarette smoke had become a part of her clothing and hair.

Allison introduced Kaleb, "one of the roommates," and then proceeded to run through all of the things they were missing in "their" apartment. I kind of felt like I had walked into a movie halfway through the screening—but just listened, and tried to act supportive of Allison's new phase of rebellion. I was confused by their relationship, though. Allison kept explaining how Kaleb was just one of her two roommates, but he kept calling her "babe." According to Allison, the other roommate was someone who worked in North Dakota's oil industry during the week, only returning to the apartment on weekends. The oil worker was the one whose name was on the lease—Kaleb the other official tenant—and Allison was Kaleb's free-loading, live-in girlfriend?

In spite of how I felt about the situation, I was polite to the young man. When he first walked in the house, and Allison introduced him, I stuck my right hand out for a handshake before he did. Then, when he complimented me for having "a nice house," I said something about how it had been a difficult road, and thanked him. Small talk with a stranger is difficult enough for me; small talk with my teenage daughter's less-than-impressive new friend was even more challenging. But I did it for Allison's sake. I wanted her to be pleased with my efforts, if nothing else.

THE DAY FRANK MOVED out of our home to his apartment across town, he had friends from work come to help him load the truck. I would have left with the kids for the day, but needed to make sure Frank and his friends didn't take more than Frank and I had agreed he was taking.

My mom told me to be nice and friendly to Frank's friends that day. I didn't think it mattered how I acted.

"Well, you don't know what Frank has been saying about you," my mother explained. "Show them you're nice and friendly. Show them the stuff Frank says about you isn't true."

AFTER SEEING THE WAY Allison looked, seeing Kaleb and his car without heat, and hearing about the apartment Allison was sharing with two guys, my steely resolve melted. By the time they left, I had packed: 1) the framed picture of Allison, Tommy, and me Allison had requested several days earlier, 2) two bath towels, two hand towels, and two washcloths, 3) several bottles of shower gels from the AVON stock I had in the basement, 4) several dishcloths, 5) four frozen pizzas from the freezer, 5) ten plastic garbage bags and twist ties, 6) two kitchen towels, 7) Allison's blanket, 8) an old kitchen sink dish drying rack from the basement, 9) a pair of scissors, 10) Allison's boxes of contact lenses from the linen closet, 11) some of her movies from the living room, since they didn't have cable, 12) half a gallon of milk from the refrigerator, and both the chocolate and strawberry Quik canisters from the cupboard, and 13) a loaf of bread, a jar of peanut butter, and a jar of jelly. The additional food items were my suggestion, after Allison moaned about not having anything to eat—and having no money to buy any food until "Monday?" she asked Kaleb.

The afternoon brought more text messages, asking for more things: a cookie sheet for cooking the pizzas, a dust pan for sweeping up the kitchen floor mess. Part of me wanted to give Allison things to help her survive. Another part of me, though, knew I shouldn't make moving out too easy for her. Helping a child set up a first apartment after college, great. Helping a child set up a first apartment after high school graduation, rather than going to college and living in the dorm, all right. But help her set up an apartment she's run to in the middle of her senior year in high school, because she's mad at me? The idea seemed preposterous.

I also wanted to be cautious about the items I let Allison take with her—because I figured they would get left behind when she changed her mind.

AFTER FRANK AND I eloped, we lived in a weird in-between-ness.

The first two nights, I was house-sitting for my boss. She and her husband were gone on a trip somewhere, and they had a brand new puppy in the basement. It was like our honeymoon, living in someone else's house together that weekend.

I remember going back to my mom's apartment, but she wouldn't let Frank stay. She was angry about our elopement. I didn't understand it at the time, but I also couldn't imagine welcoming Allison and a husband into *my* house with open arms any more than my mother was willing to embrace Frank as her son-in-law.

Frank's dad let us stay together in his house. We slept in the living room, on the sofa sleeper for a week, until Frank shipped out to basic training.

I returned to my mother's apartment when Frank went to Texas—then Oklahoma—then West Germany.

ALLISON SENT ME a text message at 6:30 p.m. on February 13th: "What is the correct way to say, 'He won't know. Not if I tell him.'"

"If I don't tell," was all I sent back.

Who is she talking to? And what doesn't she want to tell whom?

When she and Kaleb had been over, she asked to see her broken phone; she wanted to get Carl's phone number out. She managed to get Carl's sister's number, but not Carl's before the phone died again.

Has Allison been talking to Carl's sister, and now wants to keep the details of her new living situation from Carl?

How many lies is Allison creating for herself, and how many people is she hurting with those lies along the way?

Three hours later, a lengthier text from Allison—totally out of the blue. "Vic Richards was busted for drugs and alcohol last year. That's why he was working the court house last year, 'cause he was on probation and wasn't allowed to drive his police car. His daughter is in Georgia 'cause her step dad was molesting her."

Vic Richards was the policeman I developed a crush for when Allison ran away in April 2009. I had only seen him once since then: March 1st, the day Allison was arraigned on felony charges.

I stared at the message.

I paced through the house.

I read the message again.

I knew I had to respond to Allison but didn't know what to say.

My first thought was, *Damn, Allison, how did you hear this shit? Do you just ask everyone for any information about him, or what?*

My second was, *Damn, Allison, why are you bringing him up now? I haven't talked to you about him in a long time.*

My third, *Damn, Allison. Why do you want to hurt me? Here I've been so nice to you, giving you all this stuff out of my house, and this is how you repay my kindness?*

My fourth, *Happy fucking Valentine's Day to you, too, Allison! Damn. You're quite the . . .*

After ten minutes of riding the emotional waves coursing through my body, I sent back a simple, "Whoa!" in reply.

Then I walked down the hall to Tommy's bedroom, to show him the text message. Holding back the tears threatening to spill out, I simply approached him lying on his bed playing his video game, handed him my phone, and left the room.

Tommy sent Allison a text message from his phone. I never saw it, but he told me enough about it to make me feel bad for Allison. I hadn't meant for Tommy to lash back at Allison. I had wanted a hug. I had wanted someone to comfort me for another broken dream.

Five minutes later, I reached out to my girlfriends. I should have started with them, rather than Tommy, but didn't want people making fun of me for foolishly hanging onto a fantasy so long. "Okay, totally out of the blue," my text message began, "Allison sends me a text message I'm going to forward. Tommy says it's bullshit. I'm stunned either way."

Stunned if it was true, stunned if it was just a story my daughter made up to torment me.

Ever focused Lindsey responded within two minutes. "If he was busted, it should be public record."

"What the fuck is her motive, though?" I sent back to Lindsey. "She's out," as in, I had let her go. She didn't need to torment me for saying "No" to her anymore, since she had already left my house and was free of my rules.

Allison sent me another text, fifty minutes after the one about Officer Richards. "You taught my friend Jake Weber."

It took me a few minutes to adjust to the whiplash change in focus.

How was she friends with guys five minutes after meeting them? And why were none of these new friends ever girls?

I THINK I HUNG onto the fantasy of Vic Richards because it felt better to have *something* than nothing. Popular songs abound with the lyrics like, "I'd rather feel pain than nothing at all," so I knew the feeling was not uniquely mine.

But did I want to delve into his private life—even if the details were public record? My mom drilled the concept of privacy into my head on a daily basis. I spent much of my life in silence, becoming an easy victim to anyone who chose to manipulate my fears of exposure. If Allison was indeed reporting facts, she knew it would kill the dream in my head. My children knew I couldn't be involved with a drug addict again, considering what Frank dragged me through. So, what was Allison hoping to gain?

FEBRUARY 19TH, Allison sent a text asking to do laundry.

I sent the reply, "Tommy is showering, then I drop him off. Should I swing by and pick you up after that?"

Allison sent a quick "Sure" back.

I was going to see where she was living. Although she told me the directions once before, she called me on my cell phone while I was dropping Tommy off. I appreciated the gesture, and let her explain it all to me as though it was the first time.

When I got there, I sent a simple "Here?" text message. Allison came out of one of the building's many doors, laughing at my nervousness, carrying a plastic garbage bag of dirty clothes.

"You're so funny," Allison said by way of a greeting as she climbed into the car.

"Well, I wasn't sure I was at the right door" I said brightly, in my defense.

I pulled into the garage at home, and Allison jumped out of the car—leaving her bag of laundry in the car—the same way she has jumped out of the car her whole life.

"Uhm, don't forget your laundry," I said, grabbing the bag of water softener salt I had purchased on my way to pick up Allison.

She giggled, and followed me into the house.

We ate while the clothes washed. That's also when Allison pulled out the photo albums.

Allison: "I will want to get copies of some of these when I go, like away, like, to another state."

Me: "What do you mean? What state? What *are* your long term plans?"

Allison: "Oh, I don't know. Wyoming, or Texas, or great-grandma's town."

Me: "Ah. Just going by yourself, then?"

Allison: "Well, if I go to Wyoming, I'll stay with Carl. But the other places . . . I don't know."

Me: "Mmmm."

Allison: "Oh, guess who called the other day?"

Me: "I don't know, dear. Who?"

Allison: "Dad."

Me: "Oh!"

Allison: "Yeah. The first thing he said was, 'So, you're not living at home anymore, huh?'"

Me: "I wonder how he even heard. It's not like it's a big secret or anything, but I haven't even told anyone."

Allison: "He said something about the child support worker telling him."

Me: "But, how would she know? They sent that form like back in October or November, saying that you were turning eighteen, and wanting proof if you were still in school, but nobody has said anything to me since."

Allison: "Maybe the principal told them."

I don't think the school principal told Frank about Allison moving out. I believe Allison told him when he called. She probably just wanted to see what he would say. Or, hear what he might offer.

We talked, ate, and scrounged up more things for Allison to take back with her to her apartment. Mixing bowls, more clothes from her dresser, a photo album book I made for her before we moved to Wyoming, a couple of books to read. "I get so bored," she explained.

"Mom, have you done your taxes yet? Kaleb had his taxes done, and the guy said I could have gotten $2,000.00 back if I was an independent."

"Next year, we'll see how this year has gone, dear. But this year's taxes are covering last year, and in 2011 you lived in my house the entire year. You didn't even turn eighteen until December, so you are obviously my dependent."

Finally, I took the plunge into the great chasm of questions-I-want-to-ask-but-am-not-sure-I-should. "So, are you doing okay?"

"It's all right, but . . . I would come back, but my pride gets in the way."

"What do you mean?"

"I just don't want anybody saying I failed."

I think that is every human being's greatest fear. None of us wants to feel like we have failed, so we constantly make up excuses—or avoid talking about it. It's hard to admit when you've done the wrong thing; it's hard to swallow your pride. I was renewed by this tiny ray of hope. Allison had provided a slit of sunlight to peek through the clouds of my dark and dreary winter, and I secretly rejoiced.

I wanted to hug Allison, the way I have been doing since she was a toddler, and had just admitted to breaking something or hurting someone. But, I knew that would make her start crying—and I wanted to treat her like the adult she was asking to be. Rather than a hug, I told her no one would think less of her if she came back home. "No one even really knows you left, dear, since I haven't been able to talk about it."

The physical distance between us also allowed me to maintain the emotional distance to say what else I needed to say. "You know, if you come back home, though, it's going to be until you graduate. It won't be a 'thanks for letting me come home for a week—I'm going again' kind of thing. You'll also need to get a part-time job, even though I'll still drive you around and pick you up whenever you need, like it always has been. I don't have the money to keep buying you all of your stuff, *and* you need to get a job if you want to be ready to leave the *right* way the next time.

"But lots of people move back home, sweetie, and it's not because they've failed. Lots of people go home after college, or after a divorce."

As I drove Allison back to her apartment (she had been at the house for three hours), she asked if I would help her bring things in. "That way you can see the place, too."

Wow. Allison was feeling like she could trust me enough to cross another huge boundary.

It was a small apartment. It was in the basement, and it was dark. The living room had a couch, a flat screen television set on a stand, and a floor lamp that arched at about six feet. The kitchen had a refrigerator, a counter, an electric stove, and a sink full of dishes waiting to be washed. No furniture. When I opened the freezer to put in the two bags of frozen treats Allison requested from my freezer, I noticed the lone ice tray—and two bottles of alcohol.

"Those are Kaleb's brother's," Allison quickly explained.

I just smiled, shrugged and walked back to the living room.

We walked past the bathroom, but I could not see inside. Kaleb was in there, with the door closed. "I don't know if he has any pants on," Allison explained.

The last room was the bedroom Allison shared with Kaleb. A box spring and mattress, with rose-colored sheets, sat on the floor. I saw Allison's clothes hamper just inside the tiny closet, but could not see the complete width or depth of the closet. On the wall immediately to my left, there was another flat screen television. This one appeared to be larger than the one in the living room, and had video game controllers attached. They had no cable, so Allison could only watch movies. On the wall, I saw the framed picture of Allison, Tommy, and me I gave her the weekend before. There was no room for a dresser in the room.

One more closed door in the apartment—Allison explained it was the bedroom of the man who worked out of state during the week.

I was sad to see how Allison was choosing to live, but it was her choice.

Five minutes after I left, Allison sent a text. "Forgot the shampoo."

"I can swing it by tomorrow?" I offered when I got to a stoplight halfway back home.

"Yes," was Allison's quick reply.

Part of me wondered if I was still enabling her. She came to my house, did her laundry, ate some food, took some more food home with her, and now wanted me to continue supplying her with hygiene products.

If she was at college, what would I be sending in care packages? How often would I be sending care packages? Or, what would I be buying if she lived at home while taking college classes in town?

There are no easy answers.

WHEN I FOUND OUT I was pregnant with Allison, I immediately bought the book *What to Expect When You're Expecting.*

I loved the book so much, I bought the next book in the series as well: *What to Expect the First Year.*

I remember my mom always consulting her Doctor Spock book when I was a child.

I never found a surviving-the-teenage-years, or parenting-a-young-adult book that helped.

ALLISON CALLED at 6:30 p.m. February 29th. "Mom, I have a question to ask you," she began, drawing out the sentence. "Kaleb is suddenly telling me I can't have any contact with other guys, I can't text them, and he has the right to check my phone whenever he wants to."

Whether this was true or not, Allison knew controlling behavior from men was my trigger. Either way, my daughter was reaching out to me for help again.

"Where are you right now?"

"I'm at the pizza place with Katie."

It took Allison a while to form the sentence, "Can I come back home?" but she eventually asked. For the sake of our forward-going relationship, I needed her to ask, as opposed to me offering.

"Well, you understand that if you come home, it's until at least graduation. No more of this 'I'm moving out' just to move back a few weeks later, right? And, you will have to follow my rules, like come home when I tell you to come home."

Allison agreed to everything.

Did she agree too quickly, though? I mean, was she just saying whatever she felt she needed to in order to come back home for the short-term? At the moment, it didn't matter. Allison's safety was more important.

It was hard to prepare for bed, worrying about Allison, but I wouldn't be good to anyone if I didn't get a good night's sleep. I hoped she would at least call me if Kaleb tried something stupid, like hitting her.

MY DAD WAS a violent man. Because of that, I made a vow in high school: "A man only gets to hit me once," I remember saying to my two best girlfriends. "'*Gets to*,' meaning I'm gone after he does."

Frank punched a hole in the wall in the kitchen, directly to the right of my head, when we were arguing about my going back to work. Allison had come home from the daycare woman's house with a horrible looking nose. All I could figure was the woman repeatedly used a wet washcloth to aggressively wipe Allison's runny nose, not a gentle tissue.

When Frank got home that evening, and saw Allison's nose, he told me we were never going back to that woman's house again. He told me I would have to quit my job the next morning, and stay home with eighteen-month old Allison until she was ready for school.

Frank punched a hole in the wall when I told him I didn't want to quit my job.

In my mind, I defended his actions. He was angry at the incompetence of the daycare provider, upset because Allison looked so terrible. He hadn't been aiming his fist at me.

When Frank violently pushed me across the living room on the Monday of Labor Day weekend in 1997, I realized his verbal abuse had escalated to physical abuse. He had already used his *one time*.

ALTHOUGH ALLISON ASKED to come home on February 20th, she wouldn't make it until the five o'clock news started on February 22nd. Allison was home—with more bags of clothes and stuff than I remembered her taking. I guess because I saw it leave in dribs and drabs over a month's time, the return of everything in one movement made it seem like a lot.

Or, perhaps it was the fact she and Katie dropped the bags in the middle of the living room floor.

Apparently, Allison didn't tell Kaleb she was leaving. He tried calling her cell phone about five-thirty, but she wouldn't answer it. "He's going to yell at me," she explained.

By ignoring his calls, she reduced the conversation to a texted one. Allison essentially "broke up" with Kaleb with a text message.

After making it clear she had moved back home, Allison wouldn't even read or send her own text messages. She asked Katie, who was sitting on my living room couch next to Allison, to do it.

"What did he say now?" Allison kept asking Katie. "Well, tell him . . ."

I was disappointed by the lack of maturity Allison displayed, but was pleased to have her back home.

Finally, Kaleb asked to speak face-to-face with Allison. She agreed, and he drove over to meet Allison.

After Kaleb and Katie both left, Tommy, Allison, and I headed to church, as it was Ash Wednesday. While in church, though, Kaleb apparently tapped into his vein-of-anger, and sent Allison a number of angry text messages. Part of me wanted to tell Allison to put her phone away, especially after noticing some of the looks she was receiving from other people in church who saw her texting, but the other part was grateful to just have her in the pew next to me, so I let her be.

PART OF MY elementary school education was a Wednesday church service in the middle of the day, the school's policy of going to church with your family on Sundays.

On Wednesdays, we were instructed how to properly behave in church. Sit straight, eyes forward, hands in your lap. Stand on cue, kneel on cue, never stand on the furniture—kneelers included. When entering and exiting the church, your hands should be held palms together, fingers pointing towards Heaven, thumbs crossed to anchor your hands together. No talking. No exiting the service during church. Whisper to your teacher if absolutely necessary. No exceptions.

On Monday mornings, attendance-taking included Sunday morning church and Sunday school attendance.

FEBRUARY 23RD, Allison didn't miss a beat. "Can I hang out with Brad Donovan after conferences?" she asked via text message at 11:48 a.m.

Having no idea who Brad Donovan was, I simply reminded myself Allison was home—and was asking for my permission to hang out with someone after school, just the way I liked it. "Sounds good," I sent back, "if you have no homework."

Allison replied with a "None," right away.

How can you already know about homework, Allison, when the day is only half way through?

I always took the children along to conferences. I felt it was important for the teacher to get the one-on-one time with the child, explaining whatever was right or wrong in the classroom, or with their work, in front of me. That way, it didn't become a "but she hates me!" or, "he doesn't understand what I said," when I got home. Allison was in a hurry, though. Rather than taking turns, going from one of her teachers to one of Tommy's teachers, and back again, Allison wanted me to go to all of her teachers first, so she could take off with Brad. She took off, in fact, while Tommy and I were talking with one of his teachers. Allison came up behind me, whispered in my ear that she was leaving, and was gone before I could turn my head to say, "Wait."

Allison returned home shortly before the ten o'clock news started. She walked in, carrying a plastic bag with something she quickly hid in her laundry hamper under some dirty clothes, grabbed the bucket we use whenever someone feels like they are going to vomit, and headed off to bed.

Naturally, I peeked in the bag hidden in the laundry basket. Inside, I saw two cans of a new fruit-flavored malt beverage drink popular with kids, nicknamed "Knock-out in a Can," because it was a twenty-four-ounce can—twelve percent of which was alcohol. One can was empty, the other unopened.

I dumped the contents of the unopened can into the sink, and placed both cans into the recycling bin.

I QUIT MY HEAVY social drinking after hearing about the night Ben drove me all over the city. I still don't remember it.

A few years later, while Frank was away at basic training, I got a call from George, Ben's best friend. George wanted to "hang out," using Allison's words.

George bought me a bottle of my favorite wine. We sat in his basement, where Ben, George, and I had always hung out together. We shot a few games of pool, then sat on the couch because I was feeling a little too drunk.

After I threw up in his basement bathroom, George suggested I lie down.

George raped me that night.

I didn't want that kind of stuff happening to Allison.

When I got to the high school at three on February 24th, I sent both Tommy and Allison the usual text to let them know.

"I'm not at school," Allison sent right back.

"Oh?" I was proud of myself for the self-control not to tear into Allison, either through text or calling.

"I'm at Katie's, working on math and helping her with Econ."

Right. Since you're doing so well in either of those classes yourself, Allison. And, how did you manage to leave school without my permission?

Allison sent me a heads-up text message at 5:25 p.m: "Heading home."

Ten minutes later, another text. "I wasn't going to do my homework at home. So I figured it was worth going to Katie's since I did it. Obviously not in your eyes."

I hadn't said anything. I didn't understand why Allison was viciously attacking.

She was home by seven, but not for long. "Can I hang out with Kyle for a bit? He gets off work at nine."

"I suppose."

Tommy was at a school dance that ended at midnight.

"What time should I be home, then? The dance is over at midnight. I could be home by 12:30 a.m.? Or, one?"

"Or, you could be home in time for you to come with me to pick Tommy up at midnight."

"Sure, I could do that."

She sent Kyle a text, then began getting ready.

Thirty minutes later, Allison was annoyed. Kyle apparently sent a text back, saying he was too tired after all.

Not to be foiled in her plans, Allison asked, "Can I spend the night at Katie's? Since I can't spend the night tomorrow night, because I'm babysitting, this would work out better anyway."

Seeing no reason to argue, I agreed. Allison had her overnight bag packed, and was out the door in thirty minutes' time.

GROWING UP in my house, talking back to parents was forbidden. Their word was law.

Questioning a parent's decision was considered talking back.

Punishment was doled out with paddles to the buttocks. The tools utilized for such paddles were: my father's extra-large hand, complete with solid gold pinky ring on right hand, my father's leather belt, or—on rare occasion—my mother's leather-soled thin summer sandal.

I decided when I had children, I would parent with logic rather than non-negotiable law.

SUNDAY MORNING it snowed while I was in church. It snowed so much I got stuck in the driveway while trying to put the car back into the garage.

When Allison finally woke up, and made her way upstairs sometime around noon, I was already starting to think about what to make for dinner.

"Mackenzie called. Can I go snowmobiling with him, Mom?"

Rather than get into an argument with Allison, I thought about the peace and quiet a few hours of snowmobiling would bring me. "Sure."

Mackenzie pulled into the driveway about 2:30 p.m.

Allison sent a text about seven: "Well considering I'm snowed in, I don't think there will be school tomorrow."

"Snowed in where?"

"At Mackenzie's. The city doesn't plow outside town lines."

"So? Ride a snowmobile home."

"With my purse? That would ruin the leather and everything inside."

Even through a text message, I could hear Allison's signature whine. "You got there—" was all I sent in reply.

"Yeah, before it began snowing for hours. I will come home tonight, it just might take a while."

The front doorbell rang at 12:36 a.m. Mackenzie was finally dropping off Allison. She apparently tried sending text messages to Tommy, hoping he would unlock the door and let her in without me knowing, but Tommy was asleep. Her angry mother got to open the door instead.

When I began speaking, Allison cut me off with some loud, angry excuse about how they had to wait for Mackenzie's brother to return home to . . .

I stopped listening and went back to bed. Allison's laundry-list of excuses bored me.

EVERY TIME I teach a class about Argument (Aristotelian Argument), I work my way around to the questions, "What is *Truth*?" and "Who gets to define what is *True* for you, versus what is *True* for me?"

THE KIDS HAD a two-hour late start Monday, February 27th, but I did not. Rather than ride the school bus, they both accepted a ride from me at the normal time.

Shortly after ten, but before the high school day started, the school nurse called. Allison got her period and wanted to run home to change clothes. Between the sound of Allison's crying, and the memories of those same embarrassing moments in my own life, I agreed to leave work to pick her up, run her home, and then take her back to school. Before I even reached the car in the parking lot, though, Allison had sent me a text: "Can we stop at the store on the way and buy some Midol?"

"I'm not going to keep doing this, Allison," I told Allison in my calmest voice once we are in the car together. "You can't treat me like your mother one day, and ignore me as your mother another day. Today, you want me to drop everything, and risk getting in trouble at work, because you want to go home and change your pants—but last night, when you were deciding not to come home until well after curfew, you were acting like an independent adult who gets to call the shots. It doesn't work that way. You can't have it both ways."

"Well you know," Allison's voice sharpened with every word, "if you're going to shut the door like that, it will be permanent."

"Excuse me?"

"If you're not going to help me out anymore, then you're shutting the door."

"No, *you* are choosing to shut the door. I'm just saying I won't be taken advantage of. I don't play that kind of game."

"Then you're going to miss out."

I began using the "missing out" phrase to describe Frank's choice when the children were old enough to start asking tough questions. In my efforts to help them adjust to his disinterest in playing the role of a dad, I would tell them it was their father who was missing out on getting to know them. Was Allison really trying to use that same phrase against me? Although hurt by her suggestion, I didn't let it show. Instead, I matter-of-factly said, "You're right. I will be missing out. But so will you."

Allison got out of the car at the school, and walked in. It was approximately 11:30 a.m.

Another text message from Allison at 12:54 p.m. "Just bled through my second pair of pants."

When I read the text about thirty minutes later, I sent back an offer. "Wow. Can I grab some from home for you? Have a meeting at 2:00 p.m."

"No point," began Allison's response at 1:37 p.m. "Class gets over at two, then choir."

So, it's okay to have bloody pants in choir? Or, are you and Katie going to cut out of school before choir?

When I got out of the meeting, there was another text message from Allison waiting in my phone. "I'm going to get a ride from Katie," read the message she sent at 2:58 p.m.

I headed home, since Allison no longer had a house key.

I was surprised when Allison sent another text message at 3:22 p.m, rather than ringing the front door bell. "Going to pop by the store and buy Midol with my babysitting money."

Okay, but what about the pants you supposedly bled through after lunch? Was it a lie, just to get out of school early?

SIXTEEN

MARCH—BOYS, BOOZE, B.S.

Allison came home for five minutes after school on March 2nd. She was spending the weekend with Katie, but needed to "pop home to grab something," her text said.

The something was a pair of high-heeled boots, and the cable to connect her digital camera to a computer. "I'm making a Friend Album with Katie," she explained.

Shortly after six, Allison was dropped off by a boy in a white car.

Thirty minutes later, she was picked up by another boy in a pick-up truck. Were either of those boys Aaron, the boy Allison had been talking about the night before?

"Check out this text, Mom. Lacey, Aaron's ex-girlfriend, said . . ."

I didn't pay much attention to the conversation at the time, but I remember the message Aaron supposedly forwarded to Allison. The author of the original text called Allison a slut two or three times in as many sentences. "She's just mad because she thinks Aaron broke up with her because of me, but they broke up like two days ago!"

Yes, Allison, two days is plenty *of time for a girl to get over a boy breaking up with her.*

I'D REACHED the point of exhaustion with Allison. I felt like the answer to every question I asked was another story, every concern I expressed was a fight-starter, every text message Allison sent was dripping with drama, and/or a means to gain more attention.

The similarities to Frank were still enough to startle me, though.

NEAR THE END of January, Allison broke another cell phone. Rather than pay to replace her phone like I had all the other times (Tommy knows how many phones I've bought Allison over the years; I've chosen to forget), I told Allison I wouldn't call in the claim until she gave me the fifty-dollar deductible. I was surprised by the text message Allison sent at 11:06 p.m. on March 3rd. She had the money.

How? You babysat last weekend, but spent the money during the week, didn't you? Who gave you fifty dollars—and what did you give them in return?

Another text message a minute later: "I want you to meet Aaron sometime soon. I think you'll like him."

Does my liking these boys really matter to you? Or is this just something you're saying for their *benefit?*

DURING THE SPRING of 2012, I developed a variety of nicknames for Allison's revolving-door boys. Although the nicknames sound mean, I referred to them as: the-boy-of-the-week, the flavor-of-the-month, and the-five-minute-men. It was emotionally hard for me because, unlike Allison, I make lifetime friends. No sooner would I learn a boy's name, and capture a detail or two about him from Allison, so I could make conversation if I ever met him, then he'd be gone. I never knew who ended it, I just remember Allison being excited about some new boy one day—to be replaced by another new boy the next day.

Tommy tried explaining my frustration to Allison in July 2013, the first time I realized Allison was trying to drive a wedge between Tommy and me. "Allison said, 'You and Mom never liked any of the boys I ever brought home,'" Tommy reported. "I told her that wasn't true. I told her how you never got a *chance* to like them because they didn't last more than five minutes."

March 5th. Allison was standing in front of the bathroom mirror getting ready for school when I stepped into the bathroom doorway and said, "You have exactly twelve weeks of school left. If you can make it the twelve weeks, and pass these last classes, you will earn yourself a high school diploma—something your father has never done. That diploma will make you less like him and more like me."

"Dad called the other day. He said he's going to be moving to Florida this summer. And he's kicking out Brenda, because she won't get a job. Isn't that funny, though! I never thought Dad would be kicking out anyone."

Why do you focus so much on him, Allison?

I SAW A RE-RUN of a *Dr. Phil* episode about deadbeat dads in June 2013, and jotted down one comment I felt especially connected to. According to my note, Dr. Phil told the absentee father, "If your daughters have an unhealthy relationship with you, they will be vulnerable, looking for acceptance from men."

How long does the searching-behavior last?

I STARTED A LOAD of laundry instead of cooking dinner for an empty house the evening of March 6th, and needed more clothes to complete the load. I spotted Allison's weekend bag, still zipped shut, and wondered what dirty clothes were still inside. Rather than clothes, I found a quart bottle of alcohol, strewn among the q-tips, nail polish, and mouthwash still in the bag.

I grabbed the bottle of alcohol, zipped the suitcase back up, and headed directly to the kitchen sink. The bottle had ten to fourteen ounces of liquid still inside. I noticed what a pretty color it was as it headed towards the drain.

Allison was home ten minutes later, and spent the evening downstairs.

About nine-thirty she came upstairs, talking about how a male friend of hers "figured out what my therapist couldn't even figure out. He's taking Psychology this semester, and says I'm addicted to sex because I'm trying to replace the love and attention I haven't gotten from my dad."

"It's not that your therapist missed it, dear. She was trying out different theories when you first started seeing her, and you just chose to latch onto the Sex Addict label, instead of the Victim of Incest one. I've known all the way along what the situation is, but you needed to figure it out for yourself.

"You're so willing to go with guys who give you attention, because that's what you've always wanted from your dad. Rather than hold out for the long-term, loving relationship you should be focusing on, you're willing to just give guys sex, because then they pay attention to you.

"Why do you think I've been single so long? I'm holding out for that special, long-term loving relationship. I could have had plenty of guys myself, if I was willing to just have sex with them. I want a *real* relationship, with a guy who loves me for who I am, not what I do for him."

But, it's lonely, Allison. And waiting is hard.

ALLISON SENT ME a text message at 9:15 p.m. March 7th. I hadn't seen her since I dropped her off at school. "What time do you want me home?"

"The regular time."

"Okay, so I'll leave in ten minutes."

"Can you pick up milk on the way? I have five dollars to pay back—the gallon is like $3.85."

"Sure," Allison replied.

It might seem odd to people, but I had never asked either of the children to run an errand like this for me before. My mom had me walk the mile or more to the store all of the time when I was growing up, and I hated it. As a parent, I felt it was my responsibility to run the household, but I had grown tired of Allison's come-and-go-as-I-please attitude. If she wanted to act like an adult, then she could pick up some of the adult responsibilities as well.

Thirty minutes later, Allison sent a text saying, "On my way home."

Five minutes later, Allison sent another. "Aaron is going to come in and meet you for a minute, so be decent."

"Now?!" The ten o'clock news had started.

"Yeah? Just for a minute."

"Now?!" I repeated. *You just don't get it Allison. I don't want to talk to anyone at my front door after the ten o'clock news starts.*

"Yeah."

Hoping repetition would get through to Allison, I sent "Now?!" once more.

"I'll explain why when he leaves," Allison sent back.

I had no choice. Allison didn't care I was already in my pajamas—I had to meet Aaron.

Aaron stood in the entryway of the house for a minute, said "Hi," and seemed as uncomfortable as I was when I stood to shake his hand.

"He shaved off his beard, Mom, so he doesn't look like a thirty-year-old guy," was Allison's explanation.

Then Allison said, "Okay, you can leave now." Aaron said "Bye," and Allison shut the front door.

"He's really only twenty-two," Allison explained before going downstairs to bed.

Why did you joke about his looking like a thirty-year-old guy, Allison? Is he, in fact, thirty years old?

TWO DAYS LATER, Allison decided to go grocery shopping with me. Kind of like giving birth, I forgot how miserable trips to the store could be with Allison—until we were there. Comments that began as "Buy me this," and "I want that," turned into whines of "but you bought Tommy . . . , why can't I have . . . ?"

The check-out lane was no better. Allison stood in front of the cart, cell phone in hand, sending out text messages rather than unloading the shopping cart with me. When I asked her to move out of the way, she loudly groaned, rolled her eyes in the direction of the young man bagging the groceries, and walked four steps closer to him.

When we left the store, Allison ran ahead to the car. I helped the bag-boy load the bags into the trunk, because Allison was "too cold."

Home was no different. Allison walked straight into the house, leaving me to carry the bags in from the garage alone. She waited in the kitchen, though, to claim the items she had thrown into the cart.

March 14th, Allison updated me on her plans for the future.

"So Carl and I were talking on the phone last night, and he's planning on driving here for my graduation. That way, he can meet the family, and you, of course, and then he can take me back to Wyoming with him.

"I'm still going to wait to get married until next summer, because I haven't had time to plan anything—although I still have all of the phone numbers and everything."

"Wow," was all I could say at first. "So, you and Aaron aren't—"

"Oh, no. He's nice and all, but he's not much different from Daniel. He still lives at home, and isn't really planning on moving out and getting his own place for a while . . . He's still listening to everything his ex, Melinda, is saying about me.

"And Carl is done with that court stuff, by the way. They couldn't provide enough evidence, so they had to drop the charges."

How comforting. The rape charges against Carl were dismissed, for lack of evidence, just like the pornography charges against Allison were dismissed. Tommy pointed out how dismissing the charges was different from finding Carl innocent, but Allison didn't care to discuss the matter any further. She changed the subject.

Two nights later, as I brushed my teeth, Allison said she was going to "take a nap," because her friend John was coming over later.

"Later? What do you mean later, Allison? It's bedtime."

"But John doesn't get off work until like midnight, Mom. We're just going to sit outside and talk."

I tried putting my foot down, but Allison consistently ignored me. She woke me up as she tripped up the stairs at 12:45 a.m., and I asked, "What's going on?" from my bed.

She giggled, then said, "I fell going up the stairs. Sorry!"

I heard her unlock the front door, and head out.

At 2:16 a.m., I woke up because I heard voices. Half asleep, I had forgotten about the earlier conversation. I thought one of the children had left their radio on. But it wasn't music I heard, it was talking.

Then I remembered Allison telling me about John coming over. Were they downstairs in her room? How could I hear them talking? I couldn't hear actual words. I heard the rise and fall of two different mumbling voices.

I climbed out of bed, quietly walked down the hall, and paused at the top of the stairs. If they were downstairs, I expected the talking to get louder—or to see a light on—but there was nothing. It was only when I started walking towards the front door that I noticed the hood of Allison's sweatshirt through the front door window. Allison and John were sitting on the front steps, next to each other, talking.

I went to the kitchen, turned on the light over the sink, poured myself a glass of water, drank it, turned off the light, and walked back towards the living room. Since there was no acknowledgment of my presence from outside, and I was only wearing a nightshirt, I decided not to bother Allison. I went to the bathroom, and headed back to bed.

I was awake again at 4:45 a.m. Were Allison and John still sitting outside talking? I hadn't heard her come back in.

I retraced my steps from earlier, stopping at the top of the stairs first, then checking the front door—but no one was there, and the driveway was empty.

On March 18th, the kids and I were watching a movie together in the living room when Allison got a call at 7:45 p.m. "Matt wants to come over and hang out."

Five minutes later, another phone call. "Great," Allison groaned. "Now Aaron wants to come over. But Matt's already on his way.

"I asked Matt to come over," Allison explained, "because when I asked Aaron what he was doing, he said he didn't want to come all the way into town. But now that Matt's on his way, Aaron says he's changed his mind."

"Hi, Matt," Allison cooed into her cell phone. "You can really only stay for like twenty minutes, because I have to work on my math homework . . ." was all I heard before she ducked into the bathroom.

I was horrified by what my daughter was doing. Who ever taught her to play games like that? When she came out of the bathroom, I sternly told Allison I was *not* going to become her excuse for any kind of game playing. "There's no way you can tell people your mom won't let you go out because you have too much homework, because everybody already knows you don't listen to your mom anyway."

I noticed the quick smile flash across Allison's face.

"So, don't be making me part of your excuses. You didn't even ask me if it was okay if anyone came over, so don't be telling them I said they have to leave. I won't be lying for you, because when I see these boys sometime around town, I won't remember what you've even told who."

Allison went outside to wait for Matt, the smile still on her face.

Matt was only over for about twenty minutes. They came in the house, headed downstairs to Allison's room, and came back up twenty minutes later. Allison walked Matt to his car, then came back in.

Aaron arrived about fifteen minutes later.

"We're just going for a drive," Allison explained. "I should be home by ten, or ten fifteen."

"Ten would be appreciated," I replied.

"Do you know what Matt did, though?" Allison said before heading out the door. "We were by his car, and he grabbed me real tight, and said I can't leave him this summer. But, how can I stick around here, on the possibility that he'll eventually ask me out?"

"That's what some people do, honey. They wait on a possibility."

"But, I don't want to stick around and pay rent to live here, Mom. And I won't have enough money to rent a place of my own. Matt's not going to move out until he finishes school, and that's just like Daniel all over again. Besides, there's nothing I want to do around here anyway."

"You could go to school too, dear."

Allison didn't respond to that.

While Allison was out with Aaron, Lindsey sent me an update on Carl. "Had in today's paper that Allison's boy was found not guilty by a jury trial."

That's not what Allison told me. Allison said Carl's charges were dismissed, for lack of evidence.

Is Carl lying to Allison? Or, is Allison lying to me?

Lindsey's second text message had the details from the newspaper's Blotter section. "Carl . . . was found not guilty of second-degree sexual abuse of a minor by a jury."

I HAVE NO IDEA how young or old the "minor" was, or what specifically qualifies as second-degree sexual abuse in Wyoming. I don't think I would want to be dating—let alone marrying—someone who I *knew* had been to court on charges of rape, though.

Should I feel sorry for Allison? Or should I feel sorry for the many boys I believe she manipulates?

March 19th, Allison sent me a text message she was forwarding from Matt: "OMG! Your mom is my teacher next year!!"

I sent back what I thought was a cute reply: "Hope he doesn't think it's a bad thing."

(In April, his name disappeared from my class roster.)

After school, Allison asked to go over to a friend's house. "You remember how to get over to Kevin's house, don't you?"

"Kevin? Who's he?"

"Kevin, from school, Mom. He's on the football team. You took me over there before Christmas. Remember, I fell coming down the front stairs?"

"Oh, that's right."

I wanted to ask what Kevin's sudden interest was about, but knew I wouldn't get a straight answer.

I clung to the hope Allison was really trying to make friends.

Two hours after I dropped her off, Allison sent me a text message to pick her up.

When Allison got in the car, she simply said, "Kevin was starting to annoy me, so I sent you that 'Okay' text, pretending you had sent me a first one to remind me of my 6:45 appointment."

Didn't I tell you not to use me as an excuse with boys twenty-four hours ago?

MARCH 20TH, I received a text message from a number I didn't recognize. Sent at 1:15 p.m., it simply said, "Hey, it's Jake."

I ignored the text.

At 7:27 p.m., I got another text from the mysterious Jake. "Hey, Allison."

I sent a reply, "No—wrong number."

"It's Jake," he sent right back.

How had Jake gotten my number, if he was really trying to get hold of my daughter? Rather than ask Allison, I erased his messages and hoped that was the end.

THE MORNING of March 22nd Allison told me she sent Brent a text message the night before, asking why he didn't show up on the sixteenth like he planned. "He said, 'First my car broke down, then my phone broke.' Too coincidental, if you ask me."

I wanted to ask Allison why she bothered asking Brent for an excuse, but chose to focus on the feeling of vindication the conversation gave me instead. Allison was finally getting a taste of the lies she was constantly giving me. Would it change her behavior?

The text message from Allison at 11:30 a.m. suggested no. "Ron Johnson wants to hang out after I go tanning. And I've got to stay after to help Katie finish her Chem Lab. 'Cause yesterday we didn't get done 'til 4:50, and she had to figure out equations to figure out how much ammonia she needed so we need to go in after school to finish—and I'm going in to help because I have a little higher knowledge of how to do things than she does in this situation."

Who is Ron Johnson, and how do you have money for tanning, Allison?

Allison came upstairs at 10:55 p.m. on March 24th with a question on her lips. "Can I spend the night over at Katie's? Jeremy just called, and he's in the neighborhood—he would pick me up, and hang out with me until Katie's done at the dance."

"We have church tomorrow."

"He said I'll be home by nine."

"Church starts at eight-thirty. And what do you mean he said you'll be home by nine?" I strongly believed I caught her actually telling the truth: I believed she was planning on spending the night with Jeremy, not Katie.

"I'm talking about two different people," Allison said in a tired tone of voice. "I just got confused."

I gave her my verdict with a steely, no nonsense tone. "No."

"But Tommy's out . . ."

Ten minutes later, while I was pulling clothes out of the dryer, Allison called out, "Bye, Mom," from the living room, and shut the front door behind her. She hadn't been asking my permission to go; she just needed me to leave the room.

I dropped the clothes, ran to the front door—and saw Allison's blond head in the passenger seat of the car leaving my driveway.

As I headed back to the laundry, I once again saw the pile of white paper and box of markers resting on the ledge in the living room, the ledge separating the downstairs flight of stairs from the living room. When I had asked Allison about the papers earlier in the evening, she dismissed them with the comment, "They're for a flip-show Katie and I made."

Surrounded by silence, I picked up the stack of papers.

There were seventy-three sheets of paper, each with a portion of a sentence, or a single word. Each page was written in a different color marker. What was the purpose behind the effort?

Allison came home at 9:45—the next night.

She had been gone for twenty-three hours.

Perhaps this wouldn't bother every parent of an eighteen-year-old, but it bothered me. I had been down similar roads with both *my* father and *her* father.

WHEN I WAS A CHILD, my father would disappear for nearly a month at a time. I don't think my dad ever gave my mom advance warning to his disappearances. I just remember the days we would return to an empty apartment after school, and my mom would groan when she saw the bank savings account booklet on the empty kitchen table.

When Frank and I were dating, Frank would disappear for two or three days at a time. In the days and weeks that followed one of these jags, I would hear about the extensive drug use that took place during his absences.

After Frank and I were married, his disappearances slowed to only a day at a time.

How would I be able to parent Tommy in light of Allison's behavior of the past several years? I really didn't like the way Allison was disrespecting me, but didn't see a solution.

ALLISON MADE HERSELF a doctor's appointment for March 26th. She chose a time of day I was not free. I still had to call the school, though, to get her released. I didn't know who drove her from the school to the clinic. I didn't know if or when she got back to the school. I didn't know what she discussed with the doctor. All I got were text messages from Allison. The one at 10:37 a.m. said, "the $27 co-pay will be on the bill, by the way," the one at 11:16 a.m. said, "there are two prescriptions at the store needing to be picked up," for "migraine and overactive acid," and the one at 11:30 a.m. said she had "a torn ligament in the knee. Got an x-ray—they'll call with results."

The insurance for all of this was through my employer, but I was no longer consulted about any of the procedures because Allison was eighteen. I'm the parent, who will have to pay the bills (Allison doesn't have a job), but I no longer get the opportunity to veto any of the procedures before they take place.

Allison made an eye doctor appointment for herself March 27th. Just like the doctor appointment, Allison chose a time I could not join her. Once again, I had to call the school to get her released. Once again, I had no idea who was driving her to the eye doctor. I had no way of knowing if she would go back to school after the appointment.

I learned my lesson, though. During my lunch break, I drove to the eye doctor's office—to set the limits. "She's only authorized to get clear contacts, no colors. And she can't get new glasses. I'm considering just replacing the lenses in her current pair. If you want to set a box of contacts for her off to the side, I'll come back later to pay for them, thank you."

At 12:46 p.m., Allison sent me a text message I wouldn't see for another three hours: "Yeah, so I need a ride to the eye doctor. Katie sprained her calf. However that works. So, she's at home."

At 1:15 p.m., Allison sent another text message: "Never mind."

A third message at 1:35 p.m.: "So, um, I think I need crutches. I just hurt it worse walking. Insurance should pay at medical supply store by clinic."

When I read all three messages at 3:46 p.m., I was confused. Had Allison gone to the eye doctor? Was she waiting for me to pick her up from school? To clear up my confusion, I sent the message, "Where are you?"

"With Charlene," Allison replied. "I'm fine for a while."

The doctor's office called the house at 4:15 p.m. I grabbed the phone, knowing they were calling with the results from Allison's x-ray.

"Hi, may I speak to Allison, please?" the voice on the phone asked.

"I'm sorry, she's not here right now—but this is her mother."

"Okay. Would you please have her call us back as soon as possible?"

I was so angry. The doctor's office used to tell me what the test results showed, but now that Allison had reached the mystical age of eighteen, it no longer mattered who I was. I just paid the bills.

Suspecting Allison wouldn't come home until close to ten, I sent her a text message. "Call the doctor's office. They wouldn't leave the information with me."

"Okay," she replied. "What's the number?"

Allison called me back at 4:22 p.m., with the results. "They say I have a joint disfusion. The doctor says I need to stay off of it for two to three weeks, use crutches if I need to, and come back for an M.R.I. in two to three weeks if it's not better. So, would you go buy me some crutches?"

"It's called what?"

"Joint something or other. I don't know. She just said . . ." and back she went to the land of crutches, M.R.I.s, and excuses about why she couldn't get a job to pay for any of the stuff. Translation: "Me, it's all about Me, pay money for things for Me, in turn bringing more attention to Me."

"If you don't get me crutches, Mom, I'll need surgery on my knee. Surgery will cost *way* more than crutches. Do you want *that*?"

What I *wanted* was to slap the attitude right out of the sentence—and out of her body. But, I took a deep breath instead, and let the silence echo through the phone back to Allison.

"So, are you going to call the insurance to find out if they'll pay for the crutches, or am I?" Allison continued in her snooty voice.

I was tired of the game. "You can."

"What's the number?"

"It's on the back of the card."

"What card?"

"Your insurance card."

Fifteen minutes later, Allison sent a text message: "Twenty percent coinsurance. No deductible."

"They only pay twenty percent, or we do?" I sent back.

"We only pay twenty percent," was Allison's text message reply.

Allison got home just before nine. I wanted to talk to her about how the insurance worked, but she wasn't in the mood. When she yelled, "Just shut up, Mom!" I yelled back.

"What would you do if I yelled 'shut up' to you?"

"Why don't you find out."

I resisted the urge to get up to slap her face. Instead, I let her have the last word. She went downstairs for a while, came back up to make some food, and headed back down again. Thirty minutes later, she was back up, brushed her teeth, said, "I'm going downstairs now," which meant I'm-going-to-bed-now-so-you-can-come-and-tuck-me-in-for-the-night-with-a-kiss-like-you-do-every-night, and headed to bed.

I couldn't motivate myself to go down.

On March 28th, my cell phone started ringing at 12:02 p.m. The caller ID feature identified the number as the high school. Suspecting it was just the school nurse calling to tell me Allison was in her office, complaining about her knee hurting, and asking to go home for the rest of the day, I ignored the call. I have always had a hard time saying "No" to a school nurse.

When I checked the voicemail the caller left behind, I found out it was the attendance office calling. Allison had been in with a note excusing her from her study hall for the rest of the year. The signatures apparently looked similar for both student and parent. "I was just checking if this was okay with you . . ." the message said.

I called right back.

"Thanks for calling! No, I never saw that form."

"Is it okay with you, though? The policy is that the students cannot be on school grounds during that particular class period, if you sign the consent form."

Allison wants to leave the school in the middle of the day, every day, and will supposedly return for choir, her last class of the day. Riiiiight.

"No, it's really not okay with me," I replied.

"Okay, thank you. I'll mark this as rejected, and talk to her tomorrow. I think she already left for the day."

Noon. Allison is out of school for the day, and it's only noon. Wonderful. Where is she, then? What is she doing?

While I was talking with the woman from the high school, Allison sent me a text message. "Want to meet at the walk-in clinic after school?"

I wanted to tell Allison I knew she was no longer at school, but didn't want to hear another excuse. Instead, I composed my calm response. "When you asked to come back home a month ago, I outlined the terms—school being the choice over getting a job. If you're not doing the one, you need to do the other."

Allison's reply wasn't as calm. "Mom, all I would be doing is sitting there staring at the wall. There is no need to do that. It's bullshit."

I read the message, put my phone away, and walked back to the office.

Just after one o'clock, Allison started again. "So I'll meet you at the walk in clinic at like 3:00," her text message read.

I didn't respond.

At 1:45 p.m., while clearing out old text messages from my phone, I ran across the one about Katie spraining her calf. Knowing how competitive Allison is, I had a clearer picture of the sudden interest in crutches.

Was the injury phony as well?

My Internet search produced only one entry for joint disfusion: a question someone sent to a medical site Q & A column, with a reply explaining how the term is actually "joint effusion."

After reading up about joint effusion—nicknamed "water on the knee"—I sent Allison a follow up text message. "Was the doctor saying your knee is squishy?"

"She said she can feel fluid and feel it creaking."

"Yep—welcome to the family knee. You, me, Uncle Dave. It's called joint effusion, a form of arthritis."

Allison called two minutes later. "Are you home? I want to stop by really quick, and get some stuff, and Katie needs to go to the bathroom."

"Now? School's not out yet, dear."

"Mom, are we going to go through this again? I already told you . . ."

"Anyway, there's nothing you can do about your knee, except wait until you're Uncle Dave's age, and get the full knee replacement surgery like he just did. But those only have like a ten- or fifteen-year life, so in the meantime, you just learn how to walk the right way, don't twist it too much, get an elastic knee thing like I used to have . . . Getting crutches and all that won't really help. It's just something that's always with you, and it tends to hurt a bit more when the barometric pressure changes dramatically."

"Whatever. I'll be home in a little bit."

March 29th, I found out the purpose of Allison's flip-show.

"She posted you kicked her to the curb on her social networking site," Lindsey's text message began. "I emailed you her video."

"A video with flip pages I bet," I sent to Lindsey. "I saw them the day after she made them, because she left them in plain sight—as opposed to the alcohol bottles I have to dig for. She says in there she's a liar—so which part will her friends believe?"

"Anything for attention," Lindsey replied.

A STUDENT GIVING a class presentation in December 2011 showed us a video she had found online. It was a depressed young man, talking about how sad and alone he was. The topic of my student's presentation was Teen Suicide.

Allison made a video of her own, modeling the style of that young man's video. She didn't speak at all, but had a sad song playing softly in the background. I think the song was Johnny Cash singing "You Are My Sunshine."

Allison began and ended the video the same way: with a little Mona-Lisa type smile, followed by a little wave. The pages she revealed one by one contain the details of her "story."

I choose the word story, rather than life, because that's how I felt after reading the pages in the living room. The feeling grew when I watched the video Lindsey had emailed me.

I showed Tommy the video in July 2012, because he didn't understand why my attitude towards Allison had changed.

SHORTLY AFTER NOON, Allison sent me a text full of venom. "By the way, pretty sure I'm going to get suspended."

"Suspended for what?"

"Since apparently you told the lady in the attendance office that it wasn't your signature for study hall."

Just like her father, Allison wouldn't own her actions. *She* was the one who tried forging my signature, but it was *my* fault she might get suspended.

Although Allison hadn't been home for a couple of days again, by 7:39 a.m. on March 30th, she was ready to concede via text message. "I would like to focus on school. If I came home I would. I'd also be able to shower."

I was already at work by the time I read the text message at nine. Had she been trying to get into the house, to take a shower, that morning? Rather than waste time or any more effort, I sent Allison a reply at 9:10 a.m. "Why should I believe you? What makes this time different from a month ago when you agreed to the terms I presented?"

Apparently, Allison wasn't ready for the response. It took her an hour and a half to reply, but she came back with both barrels blazing. "By law to evict me from the house you have to go to the court house and pay $1,500 by the way," she sent at 10:45 a.m.

"That means if I called the cops on you, you'd go to jail," she sent at 10:49 a.m.

I wanted to explode. How dare my eighteen-year-old daughter threaten me in such a way!

Then I realized it was just an eighteen-year-old's version of a temper tantrum. Who in the world, especially in the town we were living in, was going to believe her? She had been to juvy, and she had been to court for two different cases. She'd been a runaway, and was arrested for shoplifting the day she got back home The school administrators were well aware of her story-telling, and she'd recently posted a video online admitting she was a liar.

Let her call the police. Let me have witnesses to the manipulation.

I chose to say nothing to her threats.

By 11:11 a.m., the silence was apparently too much for Allison; she tried another manipulative angle with another text message. "But I guess if you don't want me home, I'll talk to the guidance counselor and see if I have enough credit to graduate early and go out to Wyoming a.s.a.p."

I maintained my silence.

I GUESS, in all honesty, I was ready to let her go. This wasn't the way I ever imagined my daughter's senior year to pan out, but I wasn't going to spend the next two months playing her game of who-can-outsmart-whom. I was forty-seven years old. I had two jobs to pay the bills while Allison had none. The days Allison was home, she was either reclining on the couch, watching television, or heading out the door to do whatever with whomever until whenever she felt like coming home again. I didn't need the stress of a perpetual roller-coaster ride with Allison as the train's conductor.

UNABLE TO EAT dinner because I was so upset, I broke down. I couldn't stand the silence anymore. I had calmed down enough to want to talk to Allison, and hoped she had as well. I created a text message to bridge the chasm of silence between us. "I want you to be happy, I want you to love yourself, and I want to keep our relationship healthy for the long haul. If that means I have to let some physical distance grow between us while you find yourself, so be it."

Allison's venomous response came back three minutes later. "There ain't gonna be a relationship now . . . Once I leave your [sic] not gonna hear from me. Your [sic] not gonna see your grandchildren. I hope you know what your [sic] doin. Ill [sic] be there to pick up a few things in a few days."

The venom was Allison's. The threat was almost identical to what Allison's father said to me in January 1998, the day he received the divorce papers from my lawyer. The typing, though, was definitely someone else's. I had seen Allison dictate to Katie when Allison came home from her month living with Kaleb. Katie sat on the couch with Allison's phone, reading and responding to whatever text messages Kaleb sent. I didn't like being treated that disrespectfully by Allison.

"Why are you so angry?" I sent back. "What do you want that you're not getting? You've wanted to leave, you have left how many times—what do you want?"

Silence.

Shortly after eleven o'clock the morning of March 31st, I sent Allison another text message. "You honestly confuse me, sweetie. One text you say you want to come home, the next text is full of threats, the third says you are going to own your life by heading west. When I honor your decision to run your own life, you get mad all over again—for giving you the freedom you've been fighting for? I love you, sweetie. I will always love you. I've raised a strong young woman, and have confidence in your ability to accomplish whatever goals you set for yourself."

Two minutes later, Allison sent a reply. "I wanted to come home, and I'm headed out west because you won't let me come home."

"I never said you couldn't come home—you made that decision by leaving. When you came home a month ago, I presented the conditions . . ."

"I just wanted to spend the night at Katie's for one night," was Allison's ready excuse.

Sure, Allison. You just wanted to go for one night, which is why I didn't hear from you at all for two nights. So, what's your excuse for forging my signature on the paperwork at school? Or, cutting all of those classes again? Or, bringing home all of the alcohol bottles I keep finding hidden throughout the house? Or, telling people you had a miscarriage? Or, creating the online video?

I WISHED ALLISON would own *all* of her actions. Then I might want her back home. Do I let her come home, so she can at least finish out her senior year of high school? She almost has me over a barrel on this one. My mom says I need to let Allison finish. My sister says I only need to allow Allison back on my terms. Allison has no leverage. Allison will still spin the truth as she pleases.

I know these things.

I also know how life has been in our house. I know how Tommy has been affected by all of this nonsense. I know how many sleepless nights I've had. And, I know there are eight more weeks until graduation.

TWO HOURS LATER, I offered an option I could comfortably live with. I carefully prepared the text message for Allison, and sent it at 1:50 p.m. "As you can see, I have zero tolerance for the bullshit anymore. A return to my home one more time would be just that: one more time. It requires strict adherence to the rules, whether you like them or not, 100 percent attendance at school (even study hall) no more alcohol, helping out with chores, and full respect to me (I'm sick of the swearing.)"

Eight minutes later, Allison sent back her one and only response to the subject: "Funny, you just swore in the beginning of the text. That's like smoking in front of me and telling me not to smoke."

By three, I had reconsidered the one-option nature of my earlier text message, so I prepared a second text, with another option for Allison, and sent it at 3:06 p.m. "Or I can help you pack, wish you well, visit you in Wyoming, and pay the cell phone bill until the contract runs out. It's your life—I will love you no matter what you do."

A YEAR—even six months later—I would see how the push-pull dynamic of both my mother and daughter created the insecure parent I'd become.

One of the tapes playing over and over in my head was my mother's voice saying, "You need to get Allison to settle down. If she doesn't, *you're* going to be the one cleaning up the messes she makes."

Just like Frank, everything was always *my* fault—and *my* responsibility. At the time, however, I just wanted a cooperative, loving relationship with Allison.

I WAS MAKING something to eat when my cell phone received its next text message from Allison at 5:38 p.m. "Brent has in hand for me a 2800 dollar purse. My life is awesome."

It took me six minutes to process the information before I could reply with a simple "Wow."

Wow, my daughter is such a gold-digger.

Wow, my daughter is such a user.

Wow, my daughter really doesn't care about anything or anyone other than herself.

Wow, is my daughter really bi-polar or manic or something yet to be diagnosed?

Wow. Forget school, forget your mom worrying sick about you at home, forget about your high school diploma that might be swinging in the breeze. The dangling carrot of a purse from a boy who blew you off just two or three weeks ago apparently makes everything all better. Wow.

My phone rang at 7:25 p.m. The caller ID feature on my cell phone didn't register a name, but it showed a number. I recognized the area code: Chicago.

Frank. Allison's dead-beat father.

I let the call go to voicemail.

I listened to the message right away. I wanted to hear why he called, but didn't want to talk to him directly. Allison had called him, in tears. He wanted me to call him back, because he realized there are two sides to everything. He wanted to hear the other side.

How truly gracious of you, Frank. You just don't want to deal with her. You walked out of the children's lives fifteen years ago, and wouldn't even man-up when Allison ran away from home three years ago. Why would you take care of her now, when she's eighteen?

And how totally manipulative of Allison to call her father and turn on the tears.

An hour later, I decided to call Frank back. We talked for about twenty minutes, probably the longest we had talked to each other in several years. While I didn't ask for his help, or even his understanding, I explained some of the highlights living with Allison had brought me. "She took off right before midnight on New Year's eve, she moved out for the month of February, she hasn't been home in several days . . ."

Frank finally began to accept what his absence from Allison's life had meant for her—and, in turn, for me. "Wow, I had no idea."

Whether he knew it or not, Frank's words of acknowledgment meant so much to me. It was the closest Frank ever came to an apology.

"Well, I'm supposed to call her back yet tonight," Frank continued. "I get off work earlier tonight, since I worked so late last night, and I'm going to call her on my way home. I'll call you again tomorrow, and let you know how it goes."

I was annoyed by the arrogance of the absentee father who thought one simple phone call would correct fifteen years of indifference, but I was pleased by his involvement even this late in the game of parenting.

Seventeen

April—Seriously?

I TURNED MY PHONE on before church the morning of April 1st because I was eager to see if Allison was speaking to me yet. Lindsey, not Allison, had sent me a text message at 2:26 a.m. "She begged a ride to Wyoming on her social networking site, but evidently no takers."

Even though I had spent eighteen years with Allison, I was still stunned by her singular focus at times.

Allison's first text message came at 10:14 a.m. "My knee is four different colors and swelled three times its size, and I can't move my leg at all because the pain shoots from my knee to my toes."

Rather than play into her quest for attention, I sent a carefully crafted reply twenty minutes later. "Wow, sounds like you banged it up pretty good. Last night? You might want to try heat and elevation at this point, as ice only helps right after the banging."

"I didn't bang it on anything. It's been like this for weeks," Allison replied.

And then Frank called.

"She's got quite an imagination!" were Frank's opening words. No "Hello," no "How are you doing today?" Just a laugh, a long release of air, and his words of amazed exasperation.

"Yes, she does. What did she say to you?"

"She makes you out to sound like the absolute worst mother! I kept listening to her, and thinking, that doesn't sound like the Jeanette I knew when we were first married. What in the world is Allison doing?"

We talked for about twenty minutes, and a small part of me died during the conversation. If Allison was making me sound awful to her father, I shuddered to think what she'd been telling other people about me.

"She says the two of you say all kinds of mean things, and put her down. Is it possible for her to come home and just live in her bedroom for the next eight weeks without talking to her?"

Sure, Frank. That doesn't sound weird at all. A mother and daughter living together without saying a single word to each other for eight days, maybe—but eight weeks? Ridiculous.

"She also says all of her teachers hate her, of course."

Of course. Everyone hates Allison. Poor, poor, friendless Allison.

Frank got my full attention, though, when he shared his change of plans. "I told Allison, if it's an incentive for her to graduate, that I will find a way to come out there for it. And, if I have to move her here with me for the summer, I will do it—at least until I move. She won't like it, because she'll have to sleep on the couch, but . . ."

Once again, I was simultaneously relieved and annoyed by his daddy-coming-to-the-rescue attitude. On the other hand, if it helped get Allison through to graduation, I would put up with just about anything.

"Well, I'm going to call her back," Frank finally said. "I'm going to tell her that both of us agree she needs to graduate . . ."

"Yeah," I offered cheerily. "It's only eight more weeks. She can even stay a week at eight different friend's houses, just do the work to graduate."

Twenty minutes later, a text message from Lindsey snapped my head around again. "Allison posted today she went from single to being in a relationship."

A minute after Lindsey's text, Allison sent a text. "Is it okay if I come home? If I focus on school. The only thing I want is to go out like on a Saturday to hang with Katie—since I won't be skipping school."

An hour later, Allison called. "So, we're hanging out at the park, since it's such a nice day, and I thought about a bonfire. Is it okay if we come make one in the backyard and roast hotdogs and marshmallows?"

I wanted Allison home. I agreed, because it would be easier to keep the peace about small things, saving the fights for bigger concerns.

"I have nine hot dogs, but no buns," I told Allison in lieu of a Yes.

"Okay, we'll stop and get some buns."

After we hung up, I sent a text message to Lindsey. "And just like that she's coming home. Now I get to make nice-nice, like I don't know what she said about me. Eight more weeks until graduation!"

"It seems like she gets on a pity party," Lindsey sent back, "runs so she can party and do what she wants, then no one wants to take care of her any longer and let her play a victim, so she has to run home. While watching the video she made, what came to my mind is 'that's cool, one more way to manipulate a large group.'"

The group of five kids and one dog showed up at six-thirty. Allison was carrying a pair of crutches she got from Sharon, rather than using them, and left them in the living room where they would sit until school Monday morning. Allison, Katie, Sharon, and two boys I had never seen or heard of before came in the house through the front door, walked through the house, and headed out the back door.

Why not just walk around the outside of the house, you guys? The teenage brain.

According to Lindsey, while the kids were sitting in the middle of my backyard, Allison somehow managed to update her social networking site with the message, "Having a great time at my house building a fire and eating hot dogs."

HOW DOES A PARENT begin to curtail inappropriate behavior when the tools surround these kids everywhere they go? Allison didn't have a phone with Internet capability—but one or more of the friends in the backyard with her did. And, even though we didn't have Internet access in our home, one could apparently pick it up in the middle of the backyard of a house sitting on the corner lot of a dead-end, in an area far enough outside of town that everyone in the vicinity owns a number of acres as a yard. Welcome to parenting in the year 2012.

TWO HOURS LATER, everyone was gone, and Allison actually helped me clean up the grilling table—walking up and down the stairs of the house without the assistance of the crutches she was borrowing.

Biting my tongue to keep from saying what I wanted to had been a big challenge with Allison for a while. Keeping facial expressions from revealing my thoughts was an entirely new challenge Allison tested the morning of April 2nd. While getting ready for work, Allison told me about Katie having a seizure a day or two earlier. "I saved her," Allison reported. "I got her flat on the floor . . ." The explanation was given to me straight-faced, full of emotion, and so close I couldn't turn away for even a second.

"Wow," was all I could safely say.

Wow, Allison, that's quite calm and efficient of you. Wow, Allison, that's an amazing story. Do you really expect me to believe it?

"I've had seizures too," Allison continued. "That's why I've stopped drinking, Mom."

Allison stared at me some more. Was she hoping I would call her a liar? Was she hoping to start another fight?

I kept all of my energy focused on not bursting out in laughter. I wanted to tell her alcoholic black-outs weren't the same thing as seizures. I wanted to tell her she shouldn't go around making up such complicated medical lies for herself, because that's the absolute worst way to get people's attention. I wanted to tell her how full of shit she was, and that people who really *do* have seizures would get very angry with her for making up those kinds of lies about herself. I *wanted* to laugh in her face.

Allison finally broke away from the staring contest, and I woke Tommy up for school.

Allison asked for the doctor's phone number at 12:30 p.m. I wanted to ask what she needed to speak with the doctor about, but didn't think I'd get a straight answer. Like the fabled boy who cried wolf, Allison's reputation for story-telling could no longer be denied.

I sent a text message back with the doctor's phone number an hour later—when I read the text message requesting it.

THE FIRST TIME someone labeled Allison a story-teller, I was sitting in the back of the courtroom. I had been subpoenaed to testify as a witness for both the prosecution and the defense in Allison's first court case: Gregory's father was charged with contributing to the delinquency of a minor.

Based on testimony Allison gave to Officer Richards April 25, 2009, Gregory's father provided Allison with both a ride to the bus station in town, and twenty-five dollars traveling money. The police officer who questioned Gregory's father was testifying. We got to hear a tape recording of the conversation the officer had with Gregory's father. "She's always telling stories. Everyone knows it! Greg knows it, Kale knows it—everyone knows it."

If you knew she was such a storyteller, I wanted to scream, *why in the hell did you believe the line she fed you?*

I wanted to scream, but the district attorney handling the case advised Allison and me to remain stoic if we were going to sit in the courtroom. I did what the district attorney said. For two days of court proceedings, I kept my head down. I listened to a tape recording of a grown man who didn't question a fifteen-year-old girl's statement about being in the witness protection program—a fifteen-year-old girl who left school in the middle of the day, on a Friday in April, spent two hours watching a movie with his son, in the boy's bedroom, then needed a ride another four miles to the commercial bus station in town. If Allison were really in witness protection, wouldn't the police have picked her up from the school themselves? Wouldn't the police have kept her in protective custody until she left town? Wouldn't her mother be leaving with her?

I couldn't scream across the court room, but I screamed onto the yellow pad of paper I carried into court with me each morning. Every lie Gregory told to the jury, every accusation the defense attorney made about how "the *mother* knew about Allison's Internet behavior, the *mother* knew about . . . the mother *paid for* the cell phone Allison used to . . . ," every time a juror looked at me with a scowl of disapproval.

No one in court room *knew* me, as we had only been living in town a little more than a year, but they were all willing to pass judgment on me as a mother. Allison was cute, standing just a bit taller than five feet, and spoke with a soft, demure little voice.

I RECEIVED A TEXT message from Allison at 2:12 p.m. "Hi, Allison's mom," the text message began. I raced through the rest of the message. I wanted to know who had her phone, and why. "This is Katie. I am wondering if I can drop friends off at your house. After school for a bit while I work out. And if you can excuse Allison from choir. She fell in the bathroom and landed on her knee and is in extreme pain—she is screaming and crying so I'm gonna [sic] bring her home so she can nap. I'll have her home before 3:30."

Rather than deal with Katie, I pressed the "Call" option on my phone.

Allison wouldn't answer. She was forcing me to send a text message reply. "Just bring her to the house."

"We're already out at my house," the reply read.

With gritted teeth and shaking hands, I sent a terse response. "Then give me directions please."

Katie called and gave me directions to her house. By the time she called, I was already in the car, out of the garage, and pulling away from my driveway. I was going to take Allison straight to the doctor. I wanted the game to end. Rather than a general practitioner, we were going to a bone and joint specialist.

In the doctor's office, the performance escalated.

"Allison," the doctor began, "point and show me where it hurts."

She pointed.

"Allison, how does it feel when I do thi—"

"Ooooowww," the howl of pain began. A second later, the tears appeared as well.

"It hurts when I do that?" the doctor asked in disbelief.

"Yeeeeees," she moaned from the table.

"Okay, how about if I touch it he—"

"Ooooowww" again, in response to the doctor's touch.

"Okay, Allison, I want you to step down and walk for me, please."

"I can't," she moaned.

"I need you to, Allison. Just from here to the door. That's not very far."

"I caaaaaan't."

"Yes, you can."

Allison hobbled the three feet, turned around, and hobbled back.

"Okay, now I want you to squat as far as you can."

"I caaaaaan't."

"Yes, you can."

Whether she could or couldn't, she wouldn't.

"How did you say you hurt your knee again?"

"I was walking, and then went running."

"Why would you run if your knee was already hurting from walking?"

Allison shrugged her shoulders.

Finally, the doctor turned to me. "I think this has gone to a level where there is more pain being generated (pointing to the side of his head) than is actually due to the injury.

"I recommend physical therapy, to loosen the muscle stretching across the front of the knee. We could do an M.R.I., but it's not really going to show us anything, so I don't see a point. It's up to you, though, if you want an M.R.I. or not."

I didn't see the point in one either, just as I never saw the point for the extended wearing of the knee brace, or the use of crutches.

The only reason we were visiting the doctor was because I wanted an answer: did Allison really hurt her knee, or was she milking a fake injury for attention?

Before we left his office, the doctor gave me a sixteen-page packet of information describing "Patellofemoral Knee Pain." The first page described what it was, symptoms, and treatment. The other fifteen pages were full of exercises and their corresponding illustrations. We were also referred to a physical therapy office for further treatment, and asked to set up a follow-up visit with him in two weeks.

I INJURED MY right knee in high school. I like to joke with students, telling them it is my old football-knee, but I really *did* hurt it playing football. Street football. With boys from my neighborhood.

Days after I bashed my knee into the side of a parked car, it still hurt, and was red and swollen. I told the school nurse about it, but I don't know if I mentioned it to my mom or not. She was always gone, working her three jobs, and visiting my dad in the nursing home. I didn't want to add to her already heavy load.

Besides, she wouldn't have taken me to the doctor. I had been going to the doctor, and the dentist, pretty much since I was old enough to navigate my way there. Like when I chipped my front tooth in fourth grade; I walked the two blocks from the school to the dentist by myself, because my mom was working.

We got home from the doctor's office about four, and Allison slipped out the front door while I was starting a load of laundry. This time, Allison at least sent me a text message—from Katie's car—explaining she would be home in an "hour, hour and a half."

As I got ready for bed, Allison came into my room and sat on the edge of my bed. "By the way, I'm not going to Wyoming anymore. Carl has been dating this girl for a while, and he won't break up with her."

"Oh!" was all I could choke out without too much expression.

"Yeah. But Brent's going to get an apartment soon, so I'll go there. It's closer to you, and everything."

I kissed the top of her head, and walked to the bathroom to brush my teeth.

Tommy is usually more forgiving of Allison's behavior than I am, so I was surprised by his anger the morning of April 17th.

"I'm going to kill Allison," Tommy yelled as we drove home after school. "Do you know what she did today? She told Claire about all of the stuff I said to you last night, when Claire and I were fighting."

Why would Allison do that? Was Allison hoping to make Claire hate Tommy? Or, was Allison hoping to gain some dirt on Tommy she could bring back home to me? I'm not manipulative, so I don't understand the intentions behind a manipulator's actions.

DURING THE SUMMER of 2013, I noticed the wedge Allison was trying to drive between Tommy and me. She was angry with me because I wouldn't let her move back into the house, jealous of the attention Tommy was finally getting in her absence.

"So Tommy is thinking about moving to California, huh?" she cooed one day in June, after talking with Tommy the day before. "What are you going to do then, Mom?"

"I guess I'm going to figure out what I want to do with the rest of *my* life, just like you and Tommy are doing."

STATE TESTING for Tommy the morning of April 18th. Allison was a senior, so she slept in.

Just before eleven, Allison sent me a disturbing text message. "By the way, the bottle on the living room floor was found open downstairs. I forgot to dump it out and just remembered I left it in the living room by the stairs. I left in a rush this morning."

What bottle? Bottle of what? Did you bring more alcohol home, and you're now trying to make up an excuse for it being in the house because I will be home before you can remove it?

Allison purposely avoided answering any of my questions. I had to wait to see for myself when I got home.

Her trail wasn't hard to follow. Although fairly innocent, the bottle of sour cherry pop I had been hiding since our vacation to Montana a few years ago lay on the living room floor next to the remote. That bottle had been in the back of my bedroom closet in a brown paper clothing bag. The light was even still on in my bedroom—though it had been turned off when I left for work with Tommy.

What in the world possessed Allison to go digging in my bedroom closet? She didn't know about the hidden bottle of sour cherry pop. The two boxes of Girl Scout cookies are still there, the three bags of Easter candy I bought on sale are still there. What had she been after?

Tommy was staying after school, to hang out with a friend, so I asked Allison when she got into the car. "So tell me, exactly *where* did you find the bottle?"

"Downstairs."

"You already said that. But exactly where downstairs?"

"By the piano. The piano was open."

Yes, Tommy had been playing the piano for five minutes the night before, when his friend Danny stopped by. They were only downstairs for five minutes. Tommy wouldn't have had time to dig through the back of my closet with Danny. Tommy wouldn't have a reason to dig through a brown dress bag in the back of my closet. Tommy didn't even like cherry-flavored things. And I couldn't see Danny doing any of those things in the thirty minutes he stopped over to listen to music with Tommy in Tommy's bedroom.

Was this how violated Allison felt when I searched her bedroom? I didn't enjoy searching the children's rooms, but sometimes it felt necessary. I also conducted the searches as a parent, a parent trying to protect her underage children from themselves.

Ironically, most of the contraband I found over the years had been in rather plain sight: the alcohol bottles Allison left between her bed and the wall (discovered while straightening her bed), the bottles in her closet, right inside the door (discovered while hanging up clothes), or in dresser drawers (discovered while folding and putting away her clothes). Or the pack of cigarettes that fell out of a jacket pocket as I removed said jacket from the back of the dining room chair. The digital camera left on the corner of the living room coffee table the night before, and the chewing tobacco tin sitting on the top of her purse when it wasn't visible in her left back blue jean's pocket.

I wanted to know what Allison was doing digging through my bedroom closet in the first place.

I wondered if I would be able to trust her to stay at home by herself ever again.

ALLISON GOT HOME from school about six-thirty, then asked to go out with Clint about eight. She left without her purse, and came home an hour later. I didn't ask what only took an hour. I didn't want to hear another lie.

ALLISON CAME OUT of the bathroom the morning of April 20th, and gave me a glimmer of hope. "Matt's just the nicest boy," she said. "I really like him."

I kind of liked him too.

"He said last night he's kind of thinking about a relationship, but I'm so nervous. I mean, he's got his whole life all planned out, and he's so nice—I don't want to drag him down."

Wow! Allison is finally putting someone else's life and needs in front of her own? Can this be a genuine thought, or is she just setting up her next con?

Allison came home about six-thirty. The boy who gave her a ride followed her to the front door but turned and headed back to his pick-up truck when he saw me through the glass. Guess I ruined his plans?

"So I stopped and got another job application," Allison announced as she walked in the door.

I was pleased with the effort of at least picking one up, and told her.

Fifteen minutes later, Allison brought a plate of food to the dining room table where I was paying bills, and sat down to eat and talk.

"By the way," I cautiously began, "you got a piece of mail from the [local] college today. It's marked 'Urgent' or some such—"

Allison picked it up before I could finish the sentence.

She pulled out the contents, unfolded the letter, and told me it was something about registering for fall classes. "Maybe I'll take a class or two in fall," she said.

I almost fell off my chair, I was so surprised.

"I could take a class or two," Allison continued, "while I work, and stay here . . ." she drifted off.

I was almost too nervous about saying the *wrong* thing that I couldn't say anything at all.

"Oh, but it requires a check for thirty dollars." Allison set down the paperwork, and resumed eating.

"I will be happy to pay for it."

"Oh! Okay." Allison picked the paperwork back up, and began filling it out.

AT THE BEGINNING of the school year, Allison asked me to pick up an application for the local college. "Gwen is going to apply there."

"You could too, honey."

A few weeks later, Allison asked me to pick up an application for her as well.

I paid the application fee for both the local college, and the college in Montana. Allison was accepted to both, but never committed to either.

April 24th, I dropped Allison off at home after school, then drove Tommy over to the library for some Internet homework time. While I was gone, Allison did some housework.

Allison did housework?

I was pleasantly surprised when I got home and saw Allison washing the separate pieces from the top of the stove. "I found the degreaser under the sink," she announced when I stopped in the doorway between the garage and the kitchen. "It's working really well on all of this built-up grease!"

Walking through the kitchen, on my way to the dining room table to set down my purse and car keys, I noticed the vacuum cleaner sitting in the living room. "I vacuumed too," Allison announced from the kitchen sink. "And when I get done with the dishes, we can work on the graduation announcements."

What came over Allison all of the sudden?

More importantly, perhaps, what was Allison going to want as payback for all of her sudden help around the house?

April 27th, Allison and I attended the course registration day at the college. It came as a surprise, but I was thrilled Allison finally seemed to be focusing on her future in such a positive way. By the time we left the college, she had registered for three classes/nine college credits.

Walking to the car, Allison asked to go to Josh's baseball game.

Who's Josh? And why do you want to go to his game, when you never wanted to go to your brother's games?

On our drive home, she asked for "a couple of dollars, so Charlene and I can get a couple frozen pizzas tonight."

"Oh! Can I just buy you a couple of pizzas at the store?"

"For me and Charlene? But, I'm not going there until after Josh's game. Remember, I told you a couple of days ago I was going to spend the night with Charlene, because Katie isn't talking to me anymore. She's too busy with Ron lately."

I didn't want to argue. I was so happy about her registering for college classes, I wanted to continue acknowledging the grown-up she bordered on being. I handed her a five-dollar bill as we pulled into the garage, watched her pack her weekend bag, drove her back over to Josh's game, and watched her put her bag and extra boots into the back of Ryan's pickup truck before climbing into the passenger seat herself.

IN HINDSIGHT, it's easy to see the manipulation. At the time, I just saw my actions as being caring and supportive.

I TURNED MY PHONE on shortly after nine in the morning on April 28th, and read a text message Allison had sent at 7:45 a.m. "Charlene has to go work for her dad so I have to come home."

"Okay," I sent at 9:21 a.m.

"Too late now," Allison replied at 9:23 a.m. "Went out there with her 'cause I went home and knocked on the door and rang the bell."

I didn't find that believable at all. I heard the doorbell at 1:00 a.m., 2:00 a.m., 4:00 a.m.—why wouldn't I hear it at 7:00 a.m.?

I sent back a simple "?"

"You didn't wake up," Allison replied.

"So where exactly is 'work'?"

"Forty-five minutes out of town."

No town name, no direction indicated. Allison's simple excuse of being a vague "forty-five minutes out of town" somewhere was a safe kind of lie.

A minute later, another text message from Allison. "Why the '?'"

I didn't bother to reply to the question. She knew why.

Allison finally came home at four-thirty. She got out of Ryan's pickup truck rather than Charlene's. She was also wearing the same clothes she had been wearing when I dropped her off the day before. Allison muttered something about how Ryan was annoying her as she headed off to the bathroom. I sat on the couch and waited for her to come back to the living room.

"So, what happened?" I began.

Allison provided some kind of explanation, but I honestly started to glaze over when I realized it was just another story.

The end of her story was marked by a glance out the front window, before she walked back to the bathroom. When she returned to the living room, I noticed she was wearing a different low-cut tank-top.

"Josh is here," Allison announced as she made a bee-line for the front door. "Love you!"

Three hours later, she returned home for the night.

April 30th, Allison began alerting me to her plans for the afternoon just before two. "I'm going to play basketball with Kent after school. I'll be home by 5:00."

"Okay."

By four-thirty, the plans changed. "Never mind," Allison's text message began. "I'm going to stop at home to drop off my art homework and pick something up, then go to Josh's game."

"Now?"

"Yes. 'Cause there was a creepy van at the basketball court so Kent dropped me off."

I was totally confused by her message, so I tried calling Allison—but she wouldn't answer her phone.

Tommy tried from his cell phone, dialing something to prevent his number from displaying on Allison's cell phone. Sure enough, she answered the mystery call but didn't answer my call a minute earlier.

"Didn't realize you called," was the text message Allison sent me after she and Tommy talked.

Bullshit.

Allison came home at 5:15 p.m. in Ryan's pickup truck, and left five minutes later.

EIGHTEEN

MAY—THE COUNTDOWN

ALLISON CAME HOME shortly after eight on May 2nd, complaining about Josh's mom. "She doesn't want me seeing him, because she likes his old girlfriend better. In fact, they were sitting together tonight on the baseball bleachers, sending Ryan messages about what a whore I am, then laughing together about it."

I was tired of hearing this complaint. I'd heard it a hundred times over, only the names of the kids involved changed.

"Why does it matter, though?" I began. "What's so special about this boy that you have to chase after him? You do this every time. Boys should be working to get *your* attention, not the other way around."

"Mom, I've changed. I'm not chasing after him—I'm just pissed off to have this shit coming from a forty-year-old woman! And, I didn't *ask* for your opinion!" Allison yelled before she slammed the back door shut. She was heading out the swing in the backyard—her time-tested stress-relieving activity.

I had a hard time believing a forty-year-old woman would be involved in such a childish level of activity. In my head, I knew it happened; the news media reported on the older woman who bullied Phoebe Prince in Missouri through a social networking site in 2009. Cyber-bullying was blamed for Prince's suicide (January 14, 2010), and the woman was charged with the crime. But Allison tells a lot of stories.

By 8:49 p.m., the accusation of involvement still gnawed. Rather than make Allison stop swinging, I sent her a text message to ponder. "At the risk of getting yelled at some more, is it possible that someone is telling you stories? Cuz the mother could have been talking and laughing with the girl about any number of things rather than you," *you solipsistic little girl.*

"I was watching her show her the phone right as Ryan was texting her," Allison replied.

"You show me things all the time—while you ignore inbound things. Perhaps Ryan has a reason to lie?" *Perhaps Ryan hopes to keep you and Josh apart, because Ryan is jealous?*

"I was looking at the texts, Mom . . ."

"I'm not getting into this with you," Allison's next text message began. "It doesn't matter. There's a lot you don't know . . ."

True. But I do know you, Allison. I know you always want to be the center of attention, I know you stop talking to anyone who doesn't agree with you at all times.

"I was just sharing a forty-year-old Mom perspective," I sent to Allison at 8:57 p.m.

"And like I said—I didn't ask for it."

MY MOTHER WAS the second person to warn me of Allison's story-telling ability. "The things she told the Chicago police while she was in custody!" my mother exclaimed. "Allison was asked why she was running away from home, and she told them she was being abused. When pressed for an example of the abuse, all she could offer was how you were going to send her back to school after getting her frenectomy."

A frenectomy is the surgical detachment of the flap of skin connecting the upper lip to the gum line. In cases like Allison's, the flap descends too low, creating a gap between the front teeth. Removing a small triangle of skin before the age of sixteen releases the tension, and allows the teeth to move back together without the aid of braces. Once the dental assistant explained the procedure, and the suggested follow-up care of ice-packs and rest for the four to six hours following the procedure, I altered my work schedule to allow for Allison's convalescence at home. But would my pre-procedure intent to send her back to school be considered abuse?

More importantly, perhaps, why would Allison make those kinds of accusations about me?

SURPRISINGLY, ALLISON came upstairs, talking on the house phone the evening of May 4th. "Josh's mom blocked my phone number on Josh's phone. Can I get my cell phone number changed, Mom? I mean, my number has somehow gotten around to too many people I don't even know—and there are guys sending me all kinds of messages about wanting to have sex with me."

Changing a cell phone number comes with a fee. I'd changed Allison's cell phone number several times over the years, for various reasons, but told her the *last* time would *be* the last time.

I was brushing my teeth for bed when Allison approached me with another question. "Can Josh stop over tonight when he gets home from his game?"

"When?"

"He's getting back about midnight."

"No. You can see him tomorrow."

"But, we'll just sit in the driveway, Mom."

HEADING TO A FAMILY memorial service the morning of May 5th, Allison asked if she could use my phone. "I just want to text Josh during the drive," she explained, "not during the service or anything."

I didn't want to be a party to Allison's act of defiance with Josh's mom. Allison had already dragged me through some muddy places over the years.

"I don't think so, Allison. You'll be fine. You can wait to talk to him when we're back home."

"When will that be?"

"I don't know. The service is at eleven, then there might be a little lunch thing. Then we'll stop at the bookstore in town, and drive back home."

While we were in the bookstore, Allison told me Matt wanted to hang out when Allison got home. I liked Matt more than I liked Josh. Matt was a year older than Allison, whereas Josh was two years younger than Allison, and a classmate of Tommy's. (Tommy didn't like Josh. I trusted Tommy's opinion.)

Matt came over about ten minutes after we pulled into the driveway. He and Allison sat out on the front stoop talking for about twenty minutes before Allison came in to the house.

"Matt's going to come back in like ten minutes," Allison explained.

"Where's he going?"

"He's just driving around while Josh and Ryan stop over."

"What?"

"Josh and Ryan are stopping over for a minute, then Matt will come back."

My driveway suddenly felt like a revolving door. Matt left. Josh and Ryan stopped. Five minutes later, Josh and Ryan left. Matt returned. Allison got in to Matt's car. Matt drove off.

Before she left, though, Allison gave me instructions: "I will be home by nine-thirty, but Josh might call the house phone before he comes over at nine-forty-five. Don't tell him I'm with Matt, though. Just tell him I can't come to the phone."

Allison was home shortly after seven-thirty.

The house phone never rang.

APRIL 2010. Allison was in trouble at the high school again. Her phone got taken away—again—and I had to go to the principal's office to get it back. Two girls were involved in the altercation resulting in Allison's phone being taken away, but the other girl was excused. According to Allison, the girl's mom and the assistant principal, Gail, were friends.

"Allison always has so many excuses why she was using her phone during class, and I'm frankly getting tired of it," Gail began. "This time, it was because she was waiting for news from the hospital.

She said that her grandmother is waiting for a kidney donation, and she is the liaison between you and the hospital."

I couldn't help but briefly smile about how creative the story was, but could tell Gail wasn't impressed with Allison's creativity one iota.

Before I could say much more than, "Wow, she re—" Gail continued.

"In the last year and a half that she's been attending school here, I've heard about how Allison has a sugar-Daddy, who buys her whatever she wants, that Allison has a baby at home, who she gave birth to before you moved here, and how Allison's father died in an automobile accident when she was very young."

I noticed Gail wouldn't look up at me as she relayed this information. Instead, she straightened the stack of papers, the pile of pencils, and the cup of paper clips on her desk top as she spoke.

Was Gail avoiding eye-contact with me because she felt I was Allison's role model? Perhaps she thought I condoned Allison's story-telling tendencies in some way. Or, was she simply ashamed to admit to me, Allison's mother, that she no longer knew what to do with a student like Allison?

Gail retired at the end of the school year. Perhaps Allison and I were just cluttering up her last few weeks of a thirty-year career.

MAY 6TH, Tommy shared a conversation he and Allison had about Josh during the memorial lunch the day before. "She showed me a text message Jeremy sent her, asking if he could stop over for sex."

"What? Gross. She showed you the text message?"

"Yep. Then she said she was sending him a reply about how she doesn't do that anymore—she's 'saving herself.'"

I wanted to laugh. Although we never talked about it anymore, I had a feeling Allison's number of sexual partners exceeded mine. The idea of "saving" herself this late in the game seemed ludicrous.

I wanted to cry. My dreams for my daughter never included so much sexual content—especially at such a young age.

I wanted to climb into bed, and hide under the blankets. Like the monster in the closet, or hiding under the bed, I've always been afraid of what people think of me. How many people in town were already judging me for my daughter's behavior?

But, how much different would their opinions about sexual promiscuity be if Allison were a boy?

I heard Tommy continue. "She got this funny look on her face when she said it, too, so I asked her who she was 'saving herself' for. 'Is it Josh?' and she just nodded."

Allison was "saving herself" for a sixteen-year-old boy? Pride be damned, that seemed dangerous.

Without divulging the conversation Tommy and I had, I brought up the topic of sex with Allison in the afternoon. We were driving to the store so she could design some graduation party announcements at the photo kiosk. "You know," I began, "I don't care one way or the other about any of this, because you're over eighteen, but based on the way Josh's mom is blocking your phone number and stuff, I bet she would have you up for statutory rape charges if she were to find out you and Josh were having sex."

"Mom!" Allison yelled in protest.

Protest because I figured out her actual relationship with Josh? Or, protest because a child doesn't want to discuss their sex life with a parent any more than a parent wants to hear about (or imagine) their child having sex?

"The age of consent is sixteen, Mom, not that we're even having sex."

"I'm just saying . . ."

"Mom, I know the law. It's only a problem if there is a four-year difference, as in, one person under the age of sixteen and the other over twenty-one."

Sometimes I wish Allison would listen to herself. What she had described was an age difference of six years, not four! Allison likes to think of herself as a legal expert, but she only ever gets half of the information correct.

Rather than extend the argument, I let Allison have the last word—again.

I BEGAN NOTICING the stories in Wyoming. When I questioned Allison about her sexual activities at the age of thirteen, she diverted the subject by giving me a note. In the note, she wrote that her father had sexually molested her in the bathtub when she was a child, and that I could never ask her any follow up questions—nor could I confront her father, a conveniently absent parent who had moved out of our home (and lives) when Allison was three.

I honored her requests. I never asked her any follow-up questions, or made any effort to contact Frank about the matter, choosing to support Allison's need to be believed rather than satisfying my desire to have details proving her accusation to be false. I know Frank well enough to doubt his ability to perpetrate such a heinous act with his own daughter. In all honesty, I actually think he's a closeted homosexual.

But how do you tell the difference between stories and statements on a day-to-day basis?

Me: "Do you have any homework?"

Allison: "No, I did it in school."

She was in high school. I refused to be a helicopter parent, contacting the teacher every day to check if Allison was keeping up with the school work. I waited until parent-teacher conferences for a report.

Me: "Are there going to be parents chaperoning this party tonight?"

Allison: "Yep. They'll be upstairs the entire night."

She didn't share the fact that the parents were hosting their own party upstairs, where all of the guests would be drinking, and the adults would lose track of what was going on downstairs almost before I'd pulled out of the driveway.

Me: "Well, you girls enjoy the sleepover, and I'll be back to pick you up tomorrow afternoon."

Allison: "Okay, mom. Love you."

Five o'clock the next morning: "Mom, can you come pick me up? I'm really mad, cuz Macy lied. She said we were just going to stay at her house last night, but she made me come with her to meet up with her new boyfriend. I've been listening to them having sex off and on ever since we got here last night!"

After a while, the stories started to remind me of the stories Frank used to tell. "I didn't mean to smoke it! Some asshole thought it would be funny to tell me it was just marijuana."

Or, "I didn't mean to do it! You just got me so mad saying all of that stuff about not loving you. The next thing I knew, my hand was going through the drywall next to your head—I just blanked out. But you know I love you, babe! I would never mean to hurt you. I'll stop smoking pot, if that will make you happy."

ALLISON CAME UPSTAIRS the morning of May 8th, and made a glass of chocolate milk before she did anything else—her normal hangover routine.

After I dropped the kids off at school, I went back home to do some laundry. Putting her clean clothes away, I found another empty bag of candy—a bag that had been hidden in the bottom of my bedroom closet—next to a resealable cup full of a mystery liquid.

I wanted to ignore Allison's continual illegal and self-destructive behaviors, but I worried about Tommy. Was he being negatively influenced by Allison?

By eleven, I couldn't stand the debate going on in my head any longer. With no one around to talk to about my concerns, I sent a text message to Sara and Lindsey: "Do you cut the one child loose in order to save the other child?"

An hour and a half later, Lindsey replied with a simple, "Yes."

Sara asked me if I really thought Tommy wouldn't be experimenting with alcohol if Allison wasn't around. Part of me acknowledged that he probably would, but the other part was angry because of how easy Allison made it for Tommy—and perhaps how she glamorized it for him as well.

Two hours later, Allison and I were sitting in the waiting room of the doctor's office. Allison had a one o'clock appointment. I leaned toward her and quietly said, "I've taken all of the candy out of my closet, now, so please stop looking for any more."

"Well, then you can just stop digging through *my* stuff, too."

"But it's different, dear, because I'm the parent."

THE BEST STORYTELLERS, it turns out, are pretty good manipulators—of both their audience and reality. Some stories are created to cover up an ugly truth we feel unable to face, some are woven together in an attempt to heal something important that has been torn from the very seams of our existence. Some stories are told to patch a spot worn through from overuse, while others are told to build a bridge of peace and healing after the path becomes too worn down or a foundation crumbles into dust.

Should we stop telling stories? Or, is the problem located within the kinds of stories we tell, when we tell them, why we tell them, and to whom we tell them?

Allison believes herself to be a masterfully skilled storyteller. Equipped with an almost uncanny ability to alter her own reality through words, which version of her history will you trust? The profile contained within her school's "permanent file," the sealed court documents only a handful of people are allowed to see because she was a minor at the time it all took place, the memories her mother retains, or the sentences she forms for you in her texts, emails, and telephone calls? She figured out the power of tears when she was very young, and uses them now to get what she wants—even if the only thing she wants is for you to believe her latest story.

MAY 11TH, I filled out the rest of Allison's financial aid paperwork. Would she go to college in the fall? Would she get a job soon? Would she move out the day after graduation?

I decided to lightly snoop through Allison's bedroom again. I still hadn't located the last bag of Easter candy that disappeared from my bedroom closet, and was curious about her new hiding place. What I didn't expect to find were two prescription pill bottles next to the opened bag of Easter candy.

Both prescription bottles were for the same person—but not a name I recognized. One bottle had one pill; the other had five or six of what appeared to be the same pills, but the medication names on the labels were different.

I was once again traumatized by my conflicting thoughts.

1) I wanted to get rid of the pill bottles, and their contents, but knew that simple removal wouldn't put an end to anything—just as removing the vibrators didn't automatically end the sending of photographs.

2) I wanted to take my bag of candy out, so Allison knew I had found her hiding spot, but felt it would be irresponsible to leave the bottles with someone else's prescription medication behind.

3) I wanted to confront Allison with the bottles, or at least my knowledge of them, but suspected she would just make up another lie about what they were and why she had them.

4) I knew I *didn't* want to get too involved anymore, because I was still trying to get over the shame of Allison's earlier crimes.

5) I knew I needed time to think.

Allison came out of school first, claiming the front passenger seat. Tommy was forced into the back seat, as usual. Driving away from the school, Tommy began talking about an argument he was having with one of his better friends. "I don't understand what his problem is," Tommy groaned.

"Well, I talked to him like just a minute ago," Allison began, "and he said . . ."

Tommy's anger was re-ignited by Allison's comments, and launched into a re-telling of the entire encounter. Tommy thought he was safe, talking in the car to his mom and sister. Tommy didn't see Allison furiously texting someone each time Tommy finished a sentence.

Tommy hadn't learned after the fight with Claire—but I was too worried about the pill issue to remind him.

Separating the kids was the best plan, at that point. I dropped Allison off at home, then told Tommy to get back in the car with me. He reluctantly obeyed, not understanding it was in his best interest. We drove around town for a bit, talked, and Tommy calmed down. Eventually, I dropped him off at a friend's house, to play video games and hang out with other boys for a while.

Allison was swinging in the back yard when I got home. I quietly walked down to her room, and removed the prescription bottles.

By May 12th, the two-weeks-until-Allison's-graduation-party clock started up, so the kids and I took the three-hour drive to a big city. During the drive, I worked through menu-planning while Allison took notes and made shopping lists. She also made plans to visit Brent.

On our drive back home, Allison updated me. "Brent said he's going to mail my purse on Monday."

"Oh," was all I allowed myself to say.

"Yeah, he said he knows I won't stop bugging him about it until I get it, and I told him he's right."

The next morning was Mother's Day. I admit I have pretty low expectations for Mother's Day. Most years, I listened to the kids rattle around in the kitchen, fighting about who was making what for my Mother's Day special breakfast. Most years, I got breakfast, a homemade card, and a special necklace or other craft project they created in school.

Allison got out of bed for church pretty quickly that morning. I was surprised, because we only got home after eleven the night before, and she hadn't gotten up for church in more than a month—but our church was having a special senior recognition service for the high schoolers of the congregation, and Allison loved attention.

Tommy, on the other hand, wouldn't get out of bed. He was so angry at Allison all the time, he wanted no part of the service.

As we were walking out of church, Allison said, "I was going to make you something special for Mother's Day last night, but we got home so late. Should I make you some scrambled eggs when we get home?"

"No, I'm not really in the mood for breakfast. You could make me lunch!"

"Oh, okay," Allison proceeded, undaunted. "What would you like for lunch?"

"I don't know. Let's see what we have when we get home."

"I'll make you a grilled cheese sandwich," Allison said, as though she hadn't heard my wait-and-see comment.

"All right, grilled cheese on the rye bread we bought yesterday."

"That's what I was thinking," Allison said cheerily.

Allison made me a card and a grilled cheese sandwich.

Two hours later, I discovered she posted an update to her social networking site: "Made my mom a card, and a grilled cheese sandwich—I'm awesome!"

By dinnertime, I was the only one still honoring the day. I made a standard meat, starch, and vegetable dinner, with a fresh rhubarb crisp from the oven for dessert, and set the table. Sadly, no one had washed the dishes from breakfast or lunch. We had to use fancier-than-normal dishes for dinner, because they were the only ones clean.

No one spoke a single word at the table. Tommy's cell phone sat on the table, to the right of his spot, and he looked up at me when it vibrated with an inbound text message. He let it sit there, on the table, until Allison began reading—and responding to—text messages on her phone.

When Tommy was done eating, he jumped up from the table and returned to the living room to watch television. Allison sat at the table until I told her she could go—but she didn't clear her plate or glass either.

I cleared the table, loaded the dishwasher, and headed to my bedroom to read a book.

About nine, I heard the sound of Allison's voice coming from the front of the house. Walking over to my bedroom window, I saw her talking to someone in a car. Although it was too dark to see a person, I recognized the car as the one John drove from time to time.

Allison came in the house fifteen minutes later. I heard her say "Now?" to someone, then heard her go back out the door at 9:22 p.m. This time, I didn't recognize the truck parked in the driveway. Allison didn't come back in until 10:42 p.m.

Happy fucking Mother's Day.

Getting ready for school the next morning, I asked Allison about her visitors from the night before. "So, that was John and then Josh last night?"

"No, John and Ryan," Allison explained. "John came to get his invitation," but no explanation was offered for why Ryan came—or stayed so late.

After school, Allison came home with Tommy and me, stayed home all afternoon, and even invited me to join her for a walk just before six. During the walk, Allison did most of the talking. Her comments ranged from, "My friend was telling me she has my invitation hung up on her refrigerator, and her mom said how pretty I am!" to "I'm sure I'll be able to make friends at college" to "Grandma lit into me about getting a job the other day." Allison even talked about a silly conversation she and Ryan had had the night before, in his truck, and explained that he was letting her use his phone to text Josh.

"Oh, your number is still blocked?"

"Yeah. His mom said he could hang out with me, but she hasn't unblocked his phone yet. I guess she's waiting for him to ask her to unblock it.

"It was so funny, though," Allison continued. "While we were sitting in his truck, Ryan totally freaked out about a bug that was sitting on his windshield. It didn't help that he had the inside light on the whole time. He didn't want you to think we were doing anything.

"Anyway, we were sitting there talking, when he noticed this really big moth and started . . ."

I didn't find the story as funny as Allison, but enjoyed the company.

"Then he found a wood tick on his neck," Allison continued.

"Wow—good thing it wasn't a deer tick."

"I had a deer tick on me once," Allison said, turning to watch my facial reaction. "I felt it, though, and was able to get it off in time."

I don't think anyone feels a deer tick, which is what makes them so dangerous. A wood tick, yes, if you're sensitive to touch. But a deer tick? And, why was this the first time I was hearing about it? If it were true, Allison would have been telling me about it, and showing me both the tick and the spot on her skin for at least a week after she discovered it. This had all the markings of another story.

Fortunately, several blocks from home, Allison got distracted with a text message from a boy whose house we had just passed. Apparently he had been sitting on his couch, watching television, when he spotted us walking past. "What a creeper!" Allison chuckled. "Benjamin just sent me a text saying, 'Enjoying your walk? Ha ha ha.'"

I remembered the name Benjamin, but it had been a while. He graduated from the high school the year before, and attended a college about two hundred miles away. I think Allison visited with him there once—the weekend of the prom dress fight.

A block later, Allison said, "I told him to come over, but he said it would be awkward, 'because your mom's there.'"

What will be awkward? And if you're such good friends, and he lives so close, how come I've only ever heard of him once before?

"It would only be awkward if he makes it awkward," I replied.

We were only home from our walk for an hour when Allison came bounding up the stairs from the basement. "Benjamin is coming over! I'm so awesome."

She went outside to greet him, then brought him in through the front door. The two of them headed downstairs almost immediately.

An hour and a half later, I sent Allison a text message. "Weather is over—" my shorthand for, "Your friend has to go home now."

I was thrilled to see Allison staying home for a second day in a row, but my curiosity as to why was aroused. Rather than ask any questions, I proceeded with my normal routine. When I walked down to her bedroom, though, to ask Allison if she was interested in eating dinner with us, I found her sitting cross-legged in the middle of her bed, listening to the noises coming from her cell phone lying on the bed next to her.

"It's not a good time," she whispered.

"What?" I whispered back.

"It's not a good time. Mandy's drinking," she explained, while tipping her right hand up in the way she only does when describing someone drinking alcohol.

I quietly walked out of Allison's bedroom, pulled the door shut like I had found it, and walked back upstairs wondering who Mandy was, and why she was drinking on a Tuesday at six.

Twenty minutes later, Allison came upstairs. "Sorry about that, Mom. Mandy is Josh's ex-, so I sent him a text message to tell him about her drinking."

If Mandy was Josh's ex-, then why was she on the phone with Allison? Had Allison called Mandy, or had Mandy called Allison? And, just how old was Mandy? Allison was eighteen, Josh was sixteen, and the legal drinking age was twenty-one.

May 18th was Senior Skip Day. I didn't expect Allison to wake up, and come upstairs as early as she did—only a little after nine-thirty. When she asked if I knew where her bikini was, though, I lost my cheery attitude. "You know, there are lots of chores that need to be done—" *if we're going to have someone's graduation party* was the rest of the sentence, but I never got the chance to finish.

"Oh, hush up, Mom," Allison said in her snippiest voice.

I did hush up—right out to the garden, where I continued weeding the flower bed I started weeding the day before.

I stepped back into the house at eleven, to tell her something I thought about while weeding, but the sound of my voice echoed off the empty walls. Walking through the house, I spotted a little white pill on the hallway carpet, next to Allison's discarded denim shorts. Where did it come from, and what was it for?

Then I noticed the front door was hanging open. I walked over to shut it, and saw Allison—sitting in the driveway, in Ryan's truck.

I threw the mystery pill away. No point in asking Allison in front of Ryan, they would both claim it was his.

Five minutes later, Josh pulled in next to Ryan. The three kids sat and talked to each other through the open windows of their vehicles for about fifteen minutes, then left to go bridge-jumping. I told her I wished she wouldn't. I told her she didn't need to break a leg days before graduation.

She went bridge-jumping anyway.

I GREW UP in Chicago. For me, bridge-jumping means committing suicide.

For kids who live near bodies of water which bridges traverse, bridge-jumping is apparently a fun part of summer. From what I understand, the kids jump off the ledge of the bridge, landing in the water below, then climb up the bank next to the bridge—to repeat the cycle until exhausted.

I'd dropped the kids off to bridge-jump, I'd picked the kids up after bridge-jumping. I'd never stayed to watch.

Saturday, May 19th. A week until the high school graduation ceremony. And after the ceremony, I was going to have a party at my house—with lots of family, and who knew how many of Allison's friends. My mother had been to our house in this particular town a million times, my sister had been able to make the trip up from Chicago several times, but a graduation party was a new event for me. I'd heard stories from people, about how they had prepared for a graduation party (painting rooms, re-painting the exterior of the house, having carpets cleaned, landscaping the yard), but I couldn't take on those kinds of projects. I could only cook—and clean.

I needed to clean the house as though we were getting ready to sell and move.

I tried to get the children to help me clean, but Allison disappeared while Tommy and I ran to the store for more supplies.

I spent the day cleaning—by myself.

Allison complained whenever I found her alcohol and cigarettes, but she would never understand I mostly found them while doing chores *she* should have been doing.

Sunday, May 20th. No one got up to go to church with me.

I was amazed when I returned home, though. Clean dishes were air-drying in the dish rack, grocery bags with canned goods for the party were neatly lined up against the cabinets (they had been haphazardly unloaded from the trunk the night before). The hanging basket of flowers I brought home right before Mother's Day was the only thing sitting on the dining room table, and I could hear the sound of both the clothes washer and dryer running.

I walked down the hall, trying to figure out which child was suddenly so industrious—and discovered Tommy folding clean clothes in my bedroom.

"Allison's not up yet," he said with a smile. "But are you happy with what I've done?"

Happy was an understatement. Thrilled was a bit more accurate, but still felt inadequate. Ecstatic? Too much, perhaps. Ecstatic seemed to suggest "formerly considered impossible."

Tommy was waiting for an answer. "Oh, yes, dear," I simply replied while moving in for a hug. "I'm totally happy. Thank you!"

Allison came upstairs shortly after ten. Tommy immediately handed her an envelope he unearthed during his cleaning frenzy. Sent from a distant family member, I had been saving the envelope until the graduation party. I suspected it contained money, and had wanted to talk with Allison about money management before I gave it to her. My timeline was sped up thanks to Tommy's thorough cleaning.

"Well, Allison, I'm sure you are aware you're going to be getting a lot of money for graduation, so I suggest you save a lot of it. Even though you pulled all of your money out of your savings account, it's still open, and you can—"

"So what," Allison began in an angry tone of voice. "It's not like I can just cash this," she said, holding up the check.

"No, but you can put it into the bank, and after the check clears, you can pull some out. I suggest you hang onto a lot of it, though, because you're going to have to buy textbooks and . . ."

From there, the conversation spiraled into ugliness. Allison said things like, "Well, when I put that job application in last month, the lady said she would hang onto it and give me a call in August," and "I don't even want to go to college, Mom. I'm only doing it because I know I'll never hear the end of it."

"Don't go to college for me, dear. Don't go, and then blow it all off. That'll be an even bigger waste of money."

"Well, it's not like we can even afford college."

"You're right, Allison, none of us can even afford college. That's why they're called student loans. Everyone I know has them. Student loans are just a fact of life. If you don't want to go to college now, though, then don't. You could also use your graduation money to pay rent—somewhere. It's entirely up to you. The way I see it is your graduating is like a gift to *me*. In turn, my graduation gift to *you* is giving you your life. The choices are all yours—as are the outcomes of those choices. Okay? I went to college right away, because that's what my mom wanted me to do, and I didn't do really well. When I went back, so many years later, my grades were much better—but it also cost a lot more to go to college. That's why I think it's better for you to go now. But, the choice is yours."

I walked away, to continue cleaning the house. Allison went outside to swing.

Monday, May 21st. Driving the kids to school in the morning, I turned to Allison and said, "Today is the last Monday of high school for you, like forever."

Forever. No matter where her life led her, she would never be heading to high school, on a Monday, as a student, ever again.

At 10:23 a.m., a text message from Allison. "I forgot tampons. Can you bring me some? And my white jean shorts."

Allison didn't come home until about eight. "I was helping Ryan with his World War II homework. He's failing."

The excuse made as much sense as the time she claimed to be helping Katie with her chemistry homework, or her taxes.

Tuesday. I got up early because Tommy said they had to be at school for a special choir rehearsal. "Allison has to be there at 7:30, to work on the girls' song, and I have to be there at 7:45, to work on the boys' song."

After I kissed Allison awake, I whispered, "Tommy told me you have to be there early today."

Allison whispered back, "Katie's giving me a ride. She broke up with Ron, and now everyone is stabbing her in the back."

"As long as she gets you there in time for your choir thing."

I was ready to leave the house at 7:15 a.m. Allison was still blow-drying her hair.

Tommy was ready to leave the house at 7:22 a.m., but I convinced him to have a bowl of cereal. I wanted to see Allison leave.

Allison finally said, "Katie's here" at 7:25 a.m. She dashed out the front door while Tommy and I headed for the garage door.

Katie's car pulled out of the driveway as Tommy and I got into the car.

But when we pulled into the school parking lot ten minutes later, I saw Allison and Katie still sitting in Katie's car. Allison was blowing off the special choir rehearsal for the night's concert.

"Are you going to drive over there and yell at her?" Tommy asked as I drove up to the main doors.

"No, no point. She's a big girl. Let her get in trouble."

"I'm going to tell Mr . . ."

"Have a good day, sweetie. I'll see you at three! I love you."

"I love you too, Mom."

Driving home from the choir concert that evening, Allison said, "At least my friends are consistent—no one ever comes to my choir concerts."

"I'm sorry. Guess you should get new friends, eh?"

Although I said it with a smile, I really meant it. Allison either needed to pick some new friends, or she needed to learn to *be* a better friend herself—or both.

"And Matt said he can't come to my party, because he's out of town with work. He said he had to leave three weeks ago, but I saw him swimming with Kelsey and Lacey two weeks ago. I hate when people lie to me . . ." she said while climbing out of the car.

I wanted to point out how she lied all of the time too, but didn't want to make her night any worse.

Maybe she was starting to grow up.

Wednesday. I picked the kids up after school, as usual. We weren't home five minutes, though, when Ryan pulled into the driveway. Allison was back out the door, and into Ryan's truck, before I had a chance to ask her to help me continue cleaning in preparation for her party. As I walked to the door, I saw Josh pull into the driveway—then both vehicles were gone.

I didn't say anything when Allison got home at six-thirty. I didn't want to start a fight.

"So Carly got back today," Allison said as she walked into the bathroom.

I was cleaning out the sink's drain pipe. I didn't really care who Carly was, or where she just got back from.

An hour later, though, when Allison and I were in the car heading to the grocery store, I asked who Carly was.

"Josh's ex. She just got back from the treatment center."

"Oh! Why was she there? How long had she been there?"

"Her mom found out she was cutting after she and Josh broke up—and she was threatening to kill herself if they didn't get back together."

Didn't you tell me drunk-Mandy was Josh's ex- a week ago?

Thursday. Allison's last full day of high school.

Standing in the bathroom in the morning, Allison said, "I'm going to miss high school."

I bit my tongue, quickly stopping the torrent of words exploding in my brain. Miss high school? Bullshit. The entire year had been about I-can't-get-out-of-high-school-soon-enough. She just didn't want to become a nameless person in a crowd again.

I didn't hear anything from Allison until 6:51 p.m. "Are you home?" the text message read.

"Yep."

She got home about seven-fifteen, and sprawled out on the freshly vacuumed living room floor—to eat, and work on the graduation cards and gifts I had to buy for her to give her friends.

About 8:20 p.m., I noticed Allison re-applying her makeup, putting her shoes and jacket on, and pacing back and forth to the front door. "I'll be right back," she said as she ran out the front door.

Josh's car was in the driveway when I walked over to shut the front door.

The car was gone, though, when Tommy informed me it was time to take his friend home ten minutes later.

Friday. Allison's last day of high school.

When she came upstairs, I raced over to give her a kiss and a hug. "It's your last day of high school!"

"Well, we all considered yesterday to be our last day, because today, we only have classes until ten-thirty. Then we go to the auditorium, get our instructions for graduation, and then we have the picnic."

"Okay, well, it's the last day I get to drive you over for—"

"Katie's going to pick me up."

"What? You mean I don't even get to take you—"

"I'm getting a ride with Katie, Mom."

"Oh."

Neither Katie nor Allison understood the emotional significance dropping Allison off for her last day of high school held for me.

When I saw what Allison was wearing to school, though, I decided to let go. For her last day, Allison was wearing a tight little black skirt she bought with her birthday money. I'd always hated the skirt, because it was so short, tight, and had a zipper running from top to bottom in the back. To make matters worse, Allison had pulled the skirt up enough to roll the waistband down about two inches.

I spent the day cleaning again. Even though Allison was supposedly done with school by noon, she never came home. She never sent me a text message. I was angry to be doing all of the work by myself.

When I picked Tommy up from school at three, a new wave of anger rolled over me.

"Allison's not coming with us?" Tommy asked as I started to pull away from the curb.

"No. I have absolutely no idea where she even is."

"She's right there!" he said, pointing back to the school's front doors. Allison had just walked out of the front doors, flanked on either side by Katie, Ryan, and Josh.

I drove away as the anger built. I wanted to pick up the graduation cake and sandwich buns from the store before my mother and sister got into town.

Just before five, my mother and sister arrived.

Ten minutes later, my cousin and her two teenage daughters got out of their car.

Five women, four of whom live two states away, had come to help me get ready for the party—but the graduate herself couldn't be bothered.

Saturday. Graduation morning.

I woke up with a headache.

Even though I was up until well after eleven the previous night, cleaning the house, preparing the food, and getting my mother, my sister, and my kids settled in for bed, I had to get up at six to make sure everyone had time to shower and dress before the 9:00 a.m. departure.

I ate a bowl of cereal, but forgot to take an aspirin for my headache.

Katie arrived at 8:50 a.m. She was going to leave her car at our house, and ride over with Allison and me. The graduates needed to be at the building between 9:20 and 9:30 a.m.

I took pictures of the girls in their caps and gowns when they got out of the car. I took pictures of the girls adjusting Allison's cap and tassel. I gave each of the girls a hug before we parted ways at the building.

My head continued to pound.

As the crowd began to fill in around me in the auditorium, I realized how bad my headache was. I sat through the next two hours with a pounding headache, fighting the waves of nausea, talking to no one. The stadium-seating didn't make for easy conversation with anyone beyond the people sitting directly to my right and left: my mother, who can't hear out of her left ear, was sitting on my right, and an older, gray-haired gentleman I didn't know sat on my left. Tommy was sitting with the choir.

I forced myself to be alert when Allison's row of students stood up. I watched her snail's paced approach to the stage. I snapped pictures when she breached the top of the stage, was handed her diploma, and waved at me with a smile from her seat again.

My baby had officially graduated from high school.

After the ceremony, the family gathered outside for pictures. In spite of the blustery wind and chilly temperature, Allison wanted to take the pictures with the lake as her backdrop.

I drove Allison and Katie back to the house, watched Allison change shoes, and heard her say they were going to meet other friends for some ice cream really quick.

I headed downstairs, to crawl under some blankets on the futon, and fought the waves of nausea that threatened to take over.

I MISSED MOST of the graduation party, and never ate any of the food I had spent so many hours preparing.

Allison missed most of her party as well. She was home for an hour, to take some pictures and collect her gifts from the extended family. Ryan and Josh came in then, together, and whisked Allison away. I didn't hear from her again until 8:05 p.m., when she sent a text message saying she was "getting gas then coming home."

The family-party managed fine without either of us present.

WHEN I WAS finally in bed at 11:45 p.m., Allison came in and said, "Grandma gave me a really big, long hug today, and said she was so sorry that my mom wasn't even at my party."

I didn't know which one to be angrier with: my mother, for suggesting I was boycotting the party like Allison's father was, or Allison, for telling me something so hurtful after all of the hours and days I had spent—by myself—getting ready for her graduation party.

Before I could get too angry, though, a quick question entered my brain: was Allison telling the truth, or was she merely trying to manipulate me again?

Part Three

Tough Love

NINETEEN

COLLEGE

Friday, August 24, 2012

ALLISON HEADED OFF to the local college. She was going to live in the dorm with one of her high school girlfriends.

The text I sent to my sister, Sara, and Lindsey at 7:36 a.m. spoke volumes: "Finally, it's Friday morning. Lest I get nostalgic about it, she comes upstairs and glares at me because I got into the shower first. Good luck in college showering when you want, sweetie!

"Then I discovered she took the special sour cherry pop from the bag in my closet—purchased in Montana last month. Love ya, but it's time to go!"

Sunday, September 30, 2012

I was awakened in the middle of the night by the persistent ringing of the house phone. Allison was calling for a ride back to the dorm. She explained she had gone to a party with her roommate, but the roommate (her ride home) had disappeared. I was *extremely* annoyed, but also worried about the health and safety of my daughter.

"Text me the directions," I said before hanging up the house phone.

"Never mind," Allison sent to my cell phone two minutes later.

"No, you already activated the emergency call system," I angrily replied. "Give me the directions."

No response.

I called Allison's cell phone five times before she turned it off.

As I crawled back into bed at 3:11 a.m., I sent Allison one more text message: "Canceling the 'emergency call' at 3:00 a.m. is HUGE."

The next morning, Allison told me she was "roofied," then raped at the party. When I told her to call the police, she hung up.

From there, the story grew. "Hi, this is Allison's friend Hannah," began the text message I received later in the morning. "I was with her last night, and . . ."

Why was Allison's friend sending the message from Allison's phone, though?

Future versions of the party had expanded details. Allison claimed she was roofied, then gang-raped. No police report was ever filed to my knowledge, though.

Tuesday, October 23, 2012

"So, looks like I don't have an iPod," began the text message from Allison at 12:13 p.m. "The one I have, Katie gave me, and she wants it back now since she hates me."

"Why?"

"She thinks I stole something from her, but I didn't. I figure she misplaced it. She isn't coming to get it. Megan has to drop it off at her mom's."

By 7:37 p.m., Allison's mood had dramatically changed. "Ha ha, I'm such a butt."

"What did you do?"

"So Katie wanted her iPod back, right? Well . . . I threw it against the wall. A few times. It's totally demolished. Megan told Katie's mom it's been that way for a while."

That's not being a "butt," Allison, that's being a criminal.

Sunday, January 13, 2013

"Mom, I'm getting kicked out of the dorm. Can you come get me?"

"Sweetie, I told you way back when that you couldn't go to college, bomb out, and come back home without at least having a job. I will store your stuff, but not you."

"But where will I go?" she screamed into the phone.

"I have nowhere to go!" she screamed from the living room floor, several hours later.

"Guess you should have thought about that when you were skipping all those classes, dear."

"FUCK YOU, MOM!"

"Maybe it's time you get to know your dad, since that's who you've been chasing after your whole life. I'll keep your stuff here, and pay for the bus ticket to Chicago, Allison. Give him a call."

Frank didn't like the arrangement, but accepted it when he figured there was no way to wriggle out.

Monday, January 14th, I took Allison and her two bags of luggage to the bus station. I purchased the one-way ticket for the trip—the exact same bus route she took when she ran away in 2009—and gave her $100 cash travel money.

I fought back the tears as I waved good-bye, and stood frozen to the spot in front of the bus station until the bus was out of sight.

TWENTY

CHICAGO

I WAS BORN AND RAISED in Chicago. (In the city, not the suburbs.)

I still miss the food, but I don't miss the lifestyle.

My sister lives in a suburb of Chicago. My cousin and her family live in another suburb of Chicago. Every few years, I break down and drive to Chicago for a visit. One year, it was a Christmas visit, another year, an early summer visit.

I start to feel claustrophobic almost as soon as I'm close enough to the city to pick up my favorite radio station in the car.

I get nostalgic for about five minutes, driving through the old neighborhoods, before I get crabby with the traffic.

I left when I was twenty-four, but I will always consider myself to be a Chicagoan.

I LEFT THE CITY because I got too scared. I left because too many bad things happened to me there, because I never wanted to raise children there. I left the city—but I sent my daughter to live there with her father.

I felt like I lost my mind the morning I watched the bus pull out from our bus "depot" in northern Minnesota that January morning.

But I didn't know what to do with, or about her anymore. I hoped because they were so much alike, Frank would be able to convince Allison to grow up.

I hoped Allison would stop looking for love in all the wrong places.

I hoped Allison would see who Frank really was, so she would stop blaming me for the divorce.

I hoped. And prayed. A lot.

January 23, 2013

Allison sent a text message asking me to mail her birth certificate.

"Why?" I sent back.

"I need it to get a job. Dad is taking me to the Polish American Association—that's how he got the job he has now."

Frank was adopted. We are only Polish by his adoptive father's last name.

February 7, 2013

"I almost got attacked. Glad I have my pepper spray in my pocket. I used it," Allison's text message read.

Was Frank no longer paying enough attention to her?

February 14, 2013

A call from Frank at 5:10 p.m., complaining about Allison.

Why are you calling from Allison's phone, though?

A text message from Allison at 8:08 p.m.: "I'm okay, by the way."

Are reminding me you're there, because I didn't insist on speaking with you when your father called me from your cell phone?

February 19, 2013

A text from Frank at 10:49 a.m.: "Call a.s.a.p.—problem with Allison."

When I called back, Frank opened with the simple statement, "Well, your daughter got herself committed."

"Excuse me?"

"I just can't believe how stupid your daughter is. She said something to someone, and now she's stuck in there until they decide to let her go."

For Allison's sake, I listened. Frank said mean things, like, "I left her in your hands because I thought you would do a good job," "she has the mentality of a thirteen-year-old," and "it's the looney bin!" but also shared information. "Do you want the phone number for this place?" "I sent her to a place that helps women regain their lives," and "Skokie police already did a well-check on her the other day, now she makes me have to leave work again, for this!"

When Frank told me to have my insurance reject the hospital stay, though, I got angry.

Shouldn't we be doing whatever we can to help *Allison? If someone thinks it's important for her to stay there, I want her to stay.*

As soon as I got off the phone with Frank, I called the number he had given me. When no one answered, I left a message explaining who I was, and left both my home and cell phone numbers.

Someone from the hospital called the house the next day, a Wednesday, at 11:00 a.m., and left a number I was to call. I called at 3:30 p.m.—got a machine—and left my information.

An hour later, I tried calling again. Like last time, I got the machine; like last time, I left my information.

At 5:36 p.m., I sent a text message to my friends Lindsey and Sara. "It's just getting kind of creepy how much she and her dad are alike!"

Lindsey sent a text message back right away, asking if Frank had any more information.

"He claims he doesn't know," I replied. "They won't disclose information to him because she's nineteen. He claims he's getting a lawyer—but he didn't even get one for our divorce."

Sara's reply came a bit later. "Do you think they clash?"

"Frank makes it sound like they are getting along great, but they *must* clash, because the competition thing is so important—they *both* always have to 'best' everyone else, which is how he made me nuts last night. He argued that it was impossible for her to top *his* naughty teenage behavior!"

Another message from the hospital on the home phone at 11:00 a.m. on Thursday. Another attempt to return the call when I got home in the afternoon.

The silence nearly killed me.

February 24, 2013

Finally, a text message from Allison's phone at 5:19 p.m. Since Frank had been using it often—and full time while Allison was hospitalized—it took me a minute to recognize the message's sender. "Just passed your and dad's first apartment ever."

So this is how I find out you're out of the hospital? Thanks.

February 25, 2013

I was still in shock by the way Allison and Frank treated me, so decided to do something a bit more proactive for a change. "Maybe we need a defined timeline for you to sever your phone line from my account," I sent to Allison's phone at 10:59 a.m.

"Once I can afford my own phone line, yes," Allison's reply began. "I'm working hard on it."

February 27, 2013

Allison sent me a text message this afternoon, telling me about the pregnancy of one of her high school friends.

"When I saw that, I just wanted to bang my head on the keyboard. Haven't these young girls figured it out yet? Having unprotected sex leads to babies. And having babies doesn't instantly make your life better. It doesn't solve everything. It makes things way more complicated. Yeah, it's wonderful, but it closes a lot of doors at this age. And the father usually doesn't stick around. Bunch of dummies. That's what they are."

Wow. Some of the very words I've said to you when I feared you were having unprotected sex—but what a hypocrite you are, calling them *a bunch of dummies.*

March 6, 2013

I was watching a television show about out-of-control thirteen-year-old girls after work, when something reminded me of a question Allison asked the week before. So I picked up the phone and sent her a text message. "When you got out of the hospital, you asked if I was surprised by what happened. Why was that important?"

"I'm not sure," Allison replied.

"And why didn't you let me know you were out for so long?"

"Because I didn't think you cared."

Really?! After all I've said and done your entire life, you really think I didn't care? Fuck your manipulative shit.

Rather than take Allison's bait, I calmly responded, "That makes me sad. Why do you think that?"

"Because you sent me away in the first place."

I was back on familiar ground. This was full-blown Allison manipulation. My response took a few minutes—and four separate messages.

1) "I gave you everything I had for nineteen years, dear—but you always wanted your dad."
2) "So now you get to know your other parent, and you get to grow your confidence as the great young woman you are capable of being—all in the sunshine of no longer living in my shadow."
3) "I love you, sweetie, unconditionally. I hope that some day you understand what that means—and can find a partner who loves you for who you are rather than the manipulator who only 'loves' you if you do what he/she wants you to do."
4) "I'm trying to heal from a lifetime—hope you start your own healing process at a younger age than me."

Allison remained silent for three and a half hours, then sent, "If I could gift wrap the globe, I'd give you the world."

Did I win that round?

March 9, 2013

"Do you need a credit card to start a new phone contract?" Allison asked via text message at 1:38 p.m.

"I don't know."

"I don't know either. I need to change my number a.s.a.p. because the wrong person has my number."

Same stuff, different day.

"Dad doesn't want me to sign a contract, anyway."

"Then I guess you get a pay-as-you-go phone like he has, or you become the independent young woman I've always wanted you to be."

"I could do it behind his back. He doesn't know how much money I have, and I'm not planning on telling him. The money I have, over half is going to be saved, and the rest is going towards a phone. And then the money I have from a job will be split between three piles. Saving, rent, and phone."

How do you have money your dad doesn't know about? Do you have a job he doesn't know about, as well?

March 10, 2013

"Would I need your social security number to get off your account?"

This was not the first attempt Allison had made to get my social security number. She has also bragged a number of times, and to a number of people, about how she thinks our handwriting looks so much alike.

March 12, 2013

"Guess who has a job!"

Finally! Perhaps you are finally figuring it out.

"Yay! Where? Doing what? Starting when?"

March 13, 2013

I sent Allison information about an upcoming trip Tommy and I were making to Chicago. His team had a competition, and I invited Frank and Allison to join me in the cheering section.

"Okay, I can stay for a little bit," Allison's reply began, "but I have to leave for work at dinner. I got a second job."

A second job? You, who has avoided getting a job like it were the plague, suddenly has two *jobs? I must have really underestimated your dad's influence over you.*

"Where? Doing what?" I sent back.

"Working at a bar."

A bar? In Chicago? But you're only nineteen. Are you working in the back, washing dishes or something?

March 14, 2013

"I need to talk to you," Allison's text at 4:02 p.m. began. "But you can't say any of it to Dad, okay? You have to give me your word."

Are you going to tell me you're pregnant? Was the lengthy text the other day about "stupid girls" just a way to test my reaction?

"You can talk to me, dear, but we are forever both of your parents. I can't make a promise not to talk to him about something concerning my children."

"He already knows," her reply ten minutes later read. "I just don't want you yelling at him. I want us as adults to figure out what to do."

I wanted to laugh about her use of "us as adults." Most days, I felt like the *only* adult amongst us. I was typing a response when Allison called.

"Stan kicked me out. Dad's going to a shelter, and I'm staying at a friend's house, sleeping on the couch.

"Stan didn't like me coming in at four in the morning. You see, I got a job dancing. It's a nicer place, though. I don't get completely naked. I get to stay in my bra and panties. It's run by women. It's better than the place where Dad said I should go."

"You mean your dad told you to get this job?"

"No, but he's such a hypocrite. He yells at me to get a job, and then yells at me because this is what I got. Then he said, 'Well, if you're going to strip, you should at least go the Admiral. You'll get lots of money there.'

"I just don't know how else to get enough money, quickly, to get out of here. They told me I could make like $500 a night. And Fred's a nice guy. He's getting ten percent of what I make, because he's giving me a ride out there and everything. He's like my bodyguard."

You mean, he's like your pimp?

The horror didn't stop there, though. Allison kept talking.

"But I had to get out of there. Did I tell you that Stan touches me? He even asks me to give him a blow job."

I'D HEARD ACCUSATIONS like this before. Only the names change.

About six months after Allison and Daniel broke up, for instance, she told me he raped her.

"He constantly wanted sex, Mom. Even when I told him I didn't want to, he would force me to. He basically raped me."

Was this just another of Allison's justifications for having sex? She and Daniel dated for over a year. Five or six times during that year, Daniel spent the night at our house. Three or four times, Allison spent the weekend at Daniel's family's place at the lake; twenty-five or thirty times, Allison spent the weekend at Daniel's house. Would a girl voluntarily spend all that time with a boy who was raping her?

Would Stan do something like that, though? He was Frank's best friend. He was Allison's godfather.

All I can do anymore is love the child. Allison was nineteen years old when I put her on the bus to Chicago. She could easily have gotten a job at a fast food place in town, like Tommy did, and lived at home with us—but she wouldn't.

Allison had to hit her own rock-bottom before she would change.

WHILE I ABSORBED the shock of the latest word-bomb, Allison rambled on. My head was on the table for much of it. I later remembered fragments. "I just want to come home," "I miss you and Tommy so much," "I need to see a counselor," "I really need to get to the dentist."

And then Allison asked the most provocative question. "I bet you always knew I was going to do something like this, didn't you? I bet you saw it coming."

Fear, Allison. It's more accurate to say I feared something like this was coming. Unfortunately, there's nothing I can do about it—I have a seventeen-year-old son to finish raising, and this is the kind of stuff I can't have going on in my house.

Is this my fault? Did I do something to make this happen?

The pain intensified two hours later. Lindsey sent a text message asking, "Is she really working as an exotic dancer?"

Oh. No. Allison has posted the information on her social networking site. She's friends with family members. My private shame is now public fodder.

"This is not you, your choices, or life," Lindsey's next message read. "This is hers. She has chosen it."

March 15, 2013

An innocent, unrelated conversation with a co-worker brought information about a center designed to help young women get out of trouble. I nearly ran on the way back to my office, found the center's website online, then sent the information to Allison. "If you're ready to make a change, check out this online information."

"What is it?" Allison asked an hour later.

"I was told it's a place that cares. Check it out. If you're serious."

"I will."

"I love you either way."

I received no further reply from Allison.

March 17, 2013

Frank sent a text at 1:35 p.m.: "I just picked up your daughter. I'm going to put her in a youth program here. Stan doesn't want us to stay there anymore. I'm going to give her all the tools . . . I want her with me."

Just after 6:30 p.m., Allison sent a text message: "Brent found me a place for $200 a month, and jobs within walking distance. Something to consider?"

During her senior year of high school, Brent talked about coming to the house to visit a number of times, promised Allison a very expensive purse, and even suggested they live together—none of which ever panned out. Should I believe he really had a place for her?

Beyond that, I couldn't figure out why Allison kept believing Brent.

But, Brent's offer was *much* better than how Allison was living at the time.

"Well," Allison announced before I could figure out a response to send, "I'm going to stay here for a month and go to N.A. (Narcotics Anonymous) first, but then I'll go there."

Do you need N.A., or are you just trying to scam me into letting you come home?

March 19, 2013

"Got job offer at the zoo," Allison sent at 1:49 p.m.

I called Allison, to cheer. "Excellent!"

"Yeah, I go in Friday for an interview, and then . . . I had to quit both of my other jobs because I couldn't get a ride. I just want to go back home."

March 27, 2013

Frank had finally gotten a taste of what I'd been dealing with for years—and didn't seem to like it.

"She just won't change until she hits the bottom," Frank said, as though he was telling me something I didn't already know.

"So what made *you* change?" I asked.

"What? I've never changed, Jeanette," Frank said with a laugh. "I bet you've been waiting a long time to hear that, haven't you?"

Yes, and that you're sorry.

March 30, 2013

I was surprised when I received a text message from Frank at 4:39 p.m.. Unfortunately, I was not as surprised by the information. "Got my debit card stolen/used by someone she was with at the shelter, and she loses a twenty-eight-dollar bus card, all today."

Another text from Frank, an hour later: "Oh, and she goes and buys twenty dollars worth of clothes while I'm at the bank about my card. Got to love her."

Did Allison lose it, Frank—or did she sell it to someone?

April 5, 2013

Frank called, to rage. During the thirty minute, mostly one-sided call, he yelled, "She won't do anything I tell her to do!" and "She only does what she wants to do, and makes up excuses why she can't do the other stuff!"

April 9, 2013

Another text message from Frank: "This is why I can't help her. I have been waiting two days to hear from her, and she refuses help when offered."

I didn't understand what he was talking about, but I didn't ask either. I was five hundred miles away, Allison was nineteen years old, and there is a deep history of Frank's manipulation scarred into my body.

Five hours later, Frank sent me another text message. "She got kicked out of the shelter for fighting. Now she's on the street. She also never called them back like she was told to, so they won't let her back in. And she turned her phone off AGAIN, so I am done. NO MORE! She doesn't want me, or my help."

April 12, 2013

The text message Allison sent at 9:12 p.m. kind of blind-sided me: "On the bus!"

"Then I ride in a car the rest of the way," she explained in the next text message, an hour later.

Unlike Allison's trip to Chicago in January, no one gave me a heads-up call.

Who is giving you a ride, Allison? Where are you going to stay? Living in my house means full-time job, rent and/or chores, and adherence to my house-rules.

April 13, 2013

Allison came directly to the house when she got into town; she and the young man who "rescued" her stayed for an hour and a half.

As they were leaving, Allison said, "Dad said you failed in your mission."

"What mission is that?"

"The mission behind why you sent me to Chicago."

"Oh, I don't think I failed. For one thing, you finally got to know who your dad *really* is.

"You also figured out your own way back from Chicago. Sometimes a girl has got to figure out an escape route . . . Er, I mean, make travel plans."

Two hours after she left my house, a text message from Allison: "Are my sunglasses there?"

Yep, the daughter I know and love so well.

Twenty-One

The Power of Books

I AM AN AVID READER. I started voraciously reading when I was young, but lost concentration for reading when I was married. Although I was able to read quite a bit when we lived in West Germany, it was mostly an activity I participated in while Frank was away on "maneuvers" for a month at a time. My energy and desire for reading were renewed again after the divorce.

When I was young, I read to escape my reality. My dad was mean—constantly yelling at me, my mom, or my sister about something. I learned to muffle the sound by shutting my bedroom door and losing myself within the pages of a book.

I also learned how reading helps pass the time. When he was around, my dad was pretty controlling; we had to drop off and pick up my mom from her part-time job at the bank every Saturday, rather than let her take public transportation or the family car. I always sat on the left side of the back seat, behind my dad, and my sister sat on the right side, behind our mom. I was too young to tally the hours I spent waiting for my mom to get done balancing her cash drawer every Saturday. I was too engaged in whatever book I had brought along, trying to stay quietly invisible the way my dad liked us to be.

My favorite books were Nancy Drew mysteries. Nancy Drew's dad loved her, her friends thought she was great, she was pretty, and she was smart. No one could get away with telling Nancy Drew lies, because she'd always figure them out for what they were. Nancy Drew was my idol.

So why did someone give me Trixie Belden books for my tenth birthday? I wanted Nancy Drew books. No one ever bought me those. I had to check Nancy Drew books out from the library.

My sister and I walked to the library every Saturday the weather permitted. We would drop my mom off at work, go back home with my dad, then walk to the library together before returning home. We had to hurry, no dawdling allowed, because we had to get home in time to drive back over to pick my mom up from work.

The library we went to most often was just under a mile. I think it took us close to an hour to walk there and back with our arm load of books. By the time I was thirteen, I had read just about every mystery book on their shelves worth reading, and half of the books on the other shelves. I remember enjoying the biography of Amelia Erhart, but got too frustrated with *Helter Skelter* to finish it. The cabinet full of plays was fun, because reading plays stimulated my imagination more than other genres, but plays were harder to read when trapped in the car with my dad.

Occasionally, my sister and I would change our routine and head for the other library. Just over a mile walk, the route to the second library took us through some very wealthy neighborhoods. Pretty to look at, but harder to feel a connection with the families inside.

Those Saturday morning walks to the library were very important to me, though, because they provided both a break from my father and his unpredictable temper—and a means to tune him out if I wasn't the focus of his angry yelling.

Books became my best friends, essentially. Unlike kids today, who can vent their frustrations to friends through text messages, I was alone in that apartment, or that car, with my dad and his foul mood. Books were my escape.

I lost interest in books when I was married, partly because I felt the books I had been reading as a child filled my head with lies. Nancy Drew, Trixie Belden, and the Hardy Boys all had money for the cutest clothes, money to travel to great places, money to eat in "swell" restaurants. They had family who loved them, and friends who were always there when they needed help. They received accolades from adults, because they solved the mystery once again. Everything turned out great in the end for those kids. My reality was so much different.

General fiction books were no better. People who had drug or alcohol problems in the beginning of the book managed to find sobriety—and love—by the end of the book. Mysteries were good when I was young, but then I got bored when I was able to figure out a Who-Done-It plot by page 100 or 150. Romances still annoy me, because they are voyeuristic reminders of what I no longer have as a single mom.

I used to turn to books for an escape from my reality. Unfortunately, I grew up and discovered there is no escape for me.

And then I found the genre currently labeled memoir in graduate school. "Happy endings" are not required for memoirs. In fact, there aren't even "endings" in many. Memoirs are stories of strength—and survival. Memoirs are stories of surviving great odds, surviving horrific experiences, and healing from the pain of one's past.

I write my memoir(s) for myself, because I need to process through the experiences I have endured.

I write my memoir(s) for my family, so they can hopefully understand why I made the choices I did—if I'm no longer able to tell them myself.

I write my memoir(s) for you, my reader, in hopes I can help even one other person understand, forgive, and heal—because I've been very fortunate to read other people's memoirs when I needed them the most.

BEFORE ALLISON WAS arrested for sending pictures of herself over the Internet, and before she ran away from home, I used to watch news stories about young people getting into trouble. I used to watch the stories—and wondered where the parents were.

I would sit in my ivory tower, and pass judgment. "Wow, were those parents ever out of touch!"

Out of touch with their kids.

Out of touch with reality.

I sat in my ivory tower, and patted myself on the back for doing such a good job keeping my own children close.

I sat in my ivory tower, and told myself my kids were safe.

Now, I watch those news stories about young people getting into trouble, and I am sad. I'm sad for the parents, sad for the kids, for the siblings of the young people who are in trouble, or who died.

I'm sad, but I no longer judge. How can I? My daughter was one of those young people in trouble. My daughter was one of the lucky ones. She lived through the nightmare, and had a chance at a future. But my daughter and I have been judged.

We lived in a small town. I felt it everywhere I went.

Some days, I couldn't even leave the house. I didn't want to hear what they were saying.

April 2009

A story about Allison's running away made it into the big city news program the day after the on-line predator was apprehended. We lived about 300 miles away.

The news program posted many of their featured stories on their web site, and readers were able to leave comments. One reader wrote, "The apple doesn't fall too far from the tree. Wonder what the girl's parents are like."

I wanted to write back with my rebuttal. I wanted to tell the reader how hurtful the statement was.

Instead, I shut my office door and cried.

Saturday, August 11, 2012

I ran into a neighbor as I walked out to my mailbox, to retrieve the newspaper.

"How's it going?" she asked.

"Oh, it's been a long summer."

"You still have a job, don't you?"

"Yes. It's just Allison—"

"Yeah," the neighbor replied. "I keep wondering when she's going to show up pregnant. Sorry."

Sorry you said it to me? Sorry you think so low of Allison? Or, sorry for the way my daughter was turning out?

I'M HERE, but I'm isolating even more than before.

I'm here, but loving Allison is getting harder.

I'm here.

I hear.

ALLISON STAYED with the boy who picked her up from the bus in Minneapolis through June 2013.

I will probably never forget a comment the young man made one of the times they stopped over to the house in mid-May, though. I had sent Allison a text message about some cookies I had made for a church fundraiser, and asked her if she wanted to try a few before they were all gone. When she was downstairs, sifting through her collection of abandoned clothes I was still holding onto for her, the boy asked, "Can you just take her back for a couple of days? I really need a break."

After that, Allison made many attempts to return to my house. "The landlord found out I was staying there. If I don't get a job in the next week, he's going to kick us out." Two weeks later, it was "If I don't leave, the landlord said he's going to . . ."

The excuses changed, but Allison continued to live there a month or two after the threats allegedly started.

IN JULY 2013, Allison began "couch-surfing."

Basically, she stayed with various friends around town until they kicked her out.

I never asked too many questions, like how they were so willing to let her stay, or what she did to compensate them for letting her stay at their place and eat their food, because I was afraid to get sucked back into the role of Allison's caretaker. I still paid for her cell phone,

I still paid for her medical and dental insurance, I still invited her over to the house for meals. I just never let her stay the night.

WHEN ALLISON TOLD me she had registered for two classes at the college for fall 2013 semester, I was thrilled.

As a teacher at the college, I was able to request a tuition waiver for the courses themselves, but I made it clear to Allison that I couldn't pay the additional fees, or buy her the required textbooks for the courses.

A week before classes started in August, Allison said she was going to withdraw again. "I don't have the money," she whined.

Ultimately, she had hoped to postpone her student loan re-payments from fall 2012 semester by enrolling in college this fall semester.

But she also hadn't gotten a job since returning to town in April.

ALLISON JOINED ME for a drive during June 2013. I was researching a location for a novel I planned to start writing. We were in a Dairy Queen in a small town when Allison seemed to brag about having someone's credit card. "I'm not using it, though, because I think that's borderline illegal."

"It's totally illegal, dear. Why don't you give it back?"

"I'm mad at him."

"Then mail it back to the company, dear."

"Nah."

MID-JULY 2013, Allison told me she had applied for admission to another college, for spring semester, but needed me to pay the application fee.

"It's only thirty-five dollars," she whined.

I wanted to tell her I wasn't about to be paying for applications to any more colleges if she wasn't willing to get a job, but didn't want to spoil the visit. Instead, I asked her if she even knew where in the state the college was. I was surprised she wanted to go even further north and west of the town we lived in.

Three days later, she told me she was going to apply to a different college for spring semester.

LATE-JULY 2013, I got a bill in the mail from the hospital in Chicago. The bill was addressed to me, not Allison. So I called the phone number on the bill.

"Why did you send this to me? It's for my daughter."

"Well, you're the responsible party on the insurance card, ma'am."

Yes, I'm always the responsible party.

Rather than argue with the young woman, I explained that Allison didn't live with me. "I live in Minnesota."

"Oh. So should I send it to the address in the file? The address she gave us at check-in?"

"Yes. Thank you."

Good luck with that.

August 3, 2013

Seventeen-year-old Tommy and I were fighting about his behavior the night before. "You know," he yelled at me, "I'm beginning to think Allison is right."

"What do you mean?"

"The stuff she says about you yelling at her all the time—you're doing it to me now."

I tried to tell him he was wrong, but then he dropped his own word-bomb.

"Allison said when we got to Chicago, you know, when she ran away from home, that you told her she was stupid, that she should be dead, that you didn't love her anymore."

I broke down into hysterical tears that night. I've always hoped Tommy discovered the truth from my reaction to Allison's words.

But why would Allison say such hurtful things?

Why does Allison seem to hate me so much?

AT TIMES WHEN I have felt my weakest, I think about a movie I love to watch over and over: *Evan Almighty*, with Steve Carell and Morgan Freeman.

Released in 2007, the movie takes a modern spin at the Bible story of Noah and the Ark. Steve Carell becomes a "Modern Day Noah," and Morgan Freeman plays God. Disguised as the waiter, Al Mighty, Freeman's character tells Carell's wife something along the lines of, "If you pray for courage, do you think God gives you courage, or the chance to be courageous?"

After my divorce, I would often pray to God, asking Him to send me someone who would love me—just for being me.

Perhaps my children prayed for that same thing.

September 6, 2013

ALLISON SENT ME a text message, asking to stop by the house to organize her clothes. "Carl is driving up from Wyoming," the message continued. "He's going to let me stay with him."

Really? Or is this just another lie designed to make me let you come back to the house?

September 7, 2013

Allison sent a text message at 7:34 p.m., asking for directions from Wyoming.

Really? He's really coming? No one ever comes, Allison.

Is he lying to you, or are you lying to me?

September 8, 2013

Allison walked into my living room—followed by Carl.

I never really met him, as he was just a twelve-, then a thirteen-year-old kid when we lived in Wyoming.

I smiled, shook his hand, then helped Allison load up his car with her bags of clothes she had packed from various storage places in my house.

Then I took a picture of Allison and Carl together, in front of my house. They stood in the same spot Allison and Daniel had for the prom pictures in 2011.

Since it was a Sunday, Tommy, Allison, Carl, and I went out for brunch in town.

I pulled out three maps for Allison while we stood in the restaurant parking lot after eating. I showed her the route from Minnesota to North Dakota, across North Dakota, through a portion of South Dakota, and into Wyoming.

"Can you write it down, Mom?"

I wrote it down, in fewer details, then handed it to Allison.

Allison and I hugged for as long as she wanted, then I kissed her forehead and said, "I love you."

I think I surprised Carl a little bit when I moved in to hug him as well. (He was a twenty-year-old kid, after all.) I think my comment, "Good luck!" surprised him even more, though.

Ten minutes after Tommy and I got home, Allison called. "I think we got on the wrong highway. What should we do now?"

Good luck, Carl.

I love you, Allison.

Acknowledgments:

An endeavor like this is never accomplished alone.

To my first readers, Kelli and Kelly: first and foremost, I needed to know that it was worthy. Then I needed to know where it needed more work.

To my children: I hope you can forgive me for sharing so much personal stuff with the world. Releasing it was my personal path to healing.

To the many authors I had the opportunity to visit with this first summer of joining your ranks: I've taken a piece of every conversation we had, and added it to my authorial knowledge-base.

To the people who read the back of the book on my *Heart Scars* book tour, and gave me courage to continue on my journey as mother, empowered woman, and author.

Finally, to everyone at North Star Press of St. Cloud, who do so many behind-the-scenes tasks which ultimately make me shine.

Thank you all.

"Yea God!"